Contents

Preface
NICHOLAS HARRISON

Who Needs an Idea of the Literary?   1
NICHOLAS HARRISON

Performing Metaphors: The Singularity of Literary Figuration   18
DEREK ATTRIDGE

Qu'est-ce que la littérature pense? (Literary Thinking)   35
ALAIN BADIOU

The Facticity of the Literary Work   41
JEAN BESSIÈRE

Musical Thinking: Hegel and the Phenomenology of Prosody   57
SIMON JARVIS

Reflections on the Excess of Empire in Tayeb Salih's *Season of*   72
Migration to the North
BENITA PARRY

Literary Misunderstanding   91
JACQUES RANCIÈRE

A Defence of Tautology: Repetition and Difference in   104
Wordsworth's Note to 'The Thorn'
CORINNA RUSSELL

Ecrire/Writing   119
ASSIA DJEBAR

Notes on Contributors   120

For Mark
all best wishes
& thanks

Nick

Preface

The impetus for this volume came originally from my sense of the apparent divergence, and the possible convergence, of two areas in which I work: postcolonial criticism, which is written mainly in English, and certain strands of work in literary theory, often in French. Postcolonial studies is one of those areas, currently thriving in the English-speaking world, in which many critics have apparently come to view notions such as literary specificity or literary autonomy, and perhaps even literature, with suspicion. If the term 'the literary' now has a certain currency in preference to 'literature' (though in many ways the distinction is flimsy), it is partly because 'literature' is for some critics associated with dogmatic or essentialist attempts at definition and with a relatively narrow, traditional canon. In postcolonial studies — as in fields including queer theory, feminist theory and book history — many critics have reconsidered the groundings of such a canon, often in order to attack it; some have moved away from the canon; and some have abandoned entirely the study of literary texts. These intellectual shifts have taken place in a political and institutional context in which those studying and teaching literature have often come under pressure to justify their activities.

Against this backdrop there has recently been talk in postcolonial circles of 'the return of the literary'. It was tempting to include that phrase in the title of this volume; but postcolonial critics, prone to their own forms of ethnocentricity, may forget that for some critics, in different subdisciplines or different institutional and political circumstances, 'the literary' never went away, or may never return. I did not want, in any case, to work with a narrowly postcolonial focus, but to engage with what seems a much wider flourishing of new work on the literary, considered both theoretically and historically. One of the aims of this volume is simply to help disseminate some of that work — not least, in accordance with *Paragraph*'s traditions, from the French-speaking world. To that end, in addition to the references given by the essays themselves and in the Notes on Contributors, a brief bibliography at the end of this Preface lists some of the texts published in the last few years (on 'the literary' as such or on closely related issues, for instance in aesthetics), as well as a few slightly older texts that seem worth bringing to the reader's attention in this context.

Another way of describing my own starting point in assembling this collection is in terms of an idea of the literary as both deeply politically involved and as irreducible to any determinate critical or political agenda. I pursue that idea further in my own essay, and I believe that the collection as a whole may lend weight to it. But it should be added at once that not all of the contributors endorse this view, or feel a need or desire to 'defend' the literary in any such way, and they approach the literary from varied perspectives and with reference to different traditions. (Only one essay other than mine is directly concerned with postcolonial issues, and its author, Benita Parry, raises serious concerns about the literary refraction of political and historical material.) My hope, then, is that any critic dealing with literary texts will find material of interest in this collection. Indeed, one of the aims of my essay, which follows this Preface, is to argue that any critic dealing with literary texts *needs* an 'idea of the literary'. In this way, the essay is also intended to serve as an introduction to the collection as a whole, and to some of the ideas of the literary examined by other contributors. I did not feel I could synthesize or summarize their essays adequately, but I have cross-referenced them where possible, in order to suggest certain links, as well as possible disagreements, between them.

I should perhaps point out too that this volume turned out to be diverse not only in terms of authors' intellectual commitments but also, thanks to Assia Djebar's new poem, 'Ecrire'/'Writing', in terms of the genre of the contributions themselves. Several of the contributors consider literature's ability to 'think' or to 'think itself', or the paradoxes of thinking literature theoretically, and perhaps such considerations lay behind Djebar's decision to send me a poem in response to my request for an essay. In any case, this particular 'return of the literary' seems an appropriate way to close the collection.

Finally I want to thank all the contributors; the translators, Alistair Clarke, Yves Gilonne and Mary Stevens, who dealt scrupulously with some difficult material; the Bauhaus-Archiv Museum, Berlin and Phyllis Umbehr, care of the Gallery Kicken, Berlin for their kind permission to use Umbo's *Uncanny Street (Unheimliche Strasse,* 1928) on the cover; and the other friends and colleagues who have helped me with this project, especially Bob von Hallberg, Peter Hallward and Mark Treharne.

NICHOLAS HARRISON

BIBLIOGRAPHY

Note: publications mentioned in the 'Notes on Contributors' at the end of the volume are not listed here.

Badiou, Alain, 'Language, Poetry, Thought' in *Theoretical Writings*, edited and translated by Ray Brassier and Alberto Toscano (London, Continuum, 2004), 233–41.

Bahri, Deepika, *Native Intelligence: Aesthetics, Politics and Postcolonial Literature* (Minneapolis and London, University of Minnesota Press, 2003).

Beaumont Bissell, Elizabeth, editor, *The Question of Literature: The Place of the Literary in Contemporary Theory* (Manchester, Manchester University Press (Angelaki Humanities), 2002).

Bernstein, J.M., editor, *Classic and Romantic German Aesthetics* (Cambridge, Cambridge University Press, 2003).

Butler, Judith et al, *What's Left of Theory? New Work on the Politics of Literary Theory* (London and New York, Routledge, 2000).

Clark, Timothy, *Derrida, Heidegger, Blanchot: Sources of Derrida's Notion and Practice of Literature* (Cambridge University Press, 1992).

Compagnon, Antoine, *Le Démon de la théorie: littérature et sens commun* (Paris, Seuil, 1998).

De Bolla, Peter, *Art Matters* (Cambridge, Harvard University Press, 2001).

Derrida, Jacques, *Acts of literature*, edited by Derek Attridge (New York and London, Routledge, 1992).

— *Passions* (Paris, Galilée, 1993).

Domecq, Jean-Philippe, *Qui a peur de la littérature?* (Paris, Mille et une nuits, 2002).

Farrell, Frank B., *Why Does Literature Matter?* (Cornell, Cornell University Press, 2004).

Fraser, Robert, *Lifting the Sentence: On the Poetics of Postcolonial Fiction* (Manchester, Manchester University Press, 2000).

Garber, Marjorie, *A Manifesto for Literary Studies* (Seattle, Washington, Washington University Press, 2004).

Goulet, Alain, editor, *Le Littéraire, qu'est-ce que c'est?* (Caen, Presses universitaires de Caen, 2002).

Hallward, Peter, *Absolutely Postcolonial: Writing between the Singular and the Specific* (Manchester, Manchester University Press, 2001).

John, Eileen and Dominic McIver Lopes, editors, *Philosophy of Literature: Contemporary and Classic Essays: An Anthology* (Oxford, Blackwell, 2004).

Joughin, John, and Simon Malpas, editors, *The New Aestheticism* (Manchester, Manchester University Press, 2003).

Kamuf, Peggy, *The Division of Literature or the University in Deconstruction* (Chicago and London, University of Chicago Press, 1997).

Kenny, Neil, 'Books in Space and Time: Bibliomania and Early Modern Histories of Learning and "Literature" in France' *MLQ* 61:2, June 2000, 253–86.

Knapp, Steven, *Literary Interest: The Limits of Anti-Formalism* (Harvard University Press, 1993).

Lane, Jeremy, 'Pierre Bourdieu's Forgotten Aesthetic: The Politics and Poetics of Practice' *Paragraph* 27:3 (November 2004), 82–99.

Leclerc, Jean-Jacques, and Ronald Shusterman, *L'Emprise des signes: débat sur l'expérience littéraire* (Paris, Seuil, 2002).

Méchoulan, Eric, editor, *Jacques Rancière, SubStance* 33.1 (2004).

Miller, J. Hillis, *On Literature: Thinking in Action* (London and New York, Routledge, 2002).

Nancy, Jean-Luc, and Philippe Lacoue-Labarthe, *The Literary Absolute: The Theory of Literature in German Romanticism* (Albany, SUNY Press, 1988).

Pavel, Thomas, *Fictional Worlds* (Harvard University Press, 1986).

— *La Pensée du roman* (Paris, Gallimard, 2003).

Price, Leah and Seth Lerer, editors, *The History of the Book and the Idea of Literature, PMLA* 121:1 (forthcoming January 2006).

Robson, Mark, editor, *Jacques Rancière, Paragraph* 28:1 (2005).

Spivak, Gayatri Chakravorty, *Death of a Discipline* (Columbia, Columbia University Press, 2003).

Viala, Alain, editor, *De l' 'utilité' de la littérature* (Paris, Champion, 1999).

Who Needs an Idea of the Literary?

In the inaugural number of the postcolonial studies journal *Interventions*, the general editor, Robert Young, wrote:

Postcolonial writing, together with minority writing in the west and feminist writing generally, has achieved a revolution in aesthetics and aesthetic criteria of the literary, just at the moment when 'the literary' was most under attack as an outdated category of elitist institutions. In institutional terms, the impact of feminism and postcolonialism has radically changed the criteria of what makes authentic art by challenging the cultural capital from which notions of the literary were derived. Writing is now valued as much for its depiction of representative minority experience as for its aesthetic qualities.[1]

I take these remarks as my starting point because they give a sense of the recent fate of 'the literary' in certain critical fields, including postcolonial studies, and of the suspicions and anxieties that circulate around that notion at present: it has come to be associated with particular (challengeable, but here unspecified) forms of 'cultural capital'; it is seen as 'an outdated category of elitist institutions'; and the way writing is 'valued' has changed. But despite their bold tone, Young's remarks are of interest to me also because they are ambivalent: it is not clear whether, during the ongoing 'revolution in aesthetics and aesthetic criteria', as Young describes it, 'the literary', seemingly already under attack when postcolonialism came along, has been redeemed or destroyed. The aim of this essay is to offer greater clarity about what is at stake, politically and aesthetically, in the shift Young depicts. The issues in play include pedagogy, models of reading, and the literary as such; and, through the example of postcolonial studies, I will argue that ideas of the literary are of interest, and necessary, even to those whose primary concerns and goals lie elsewhere.

Like many commentaries on the literary, Young's statement is somewhat prescriptive; and, although it raises broad political considerations, its ambit is primarily academic, in that it concerns the place of 'the literary' in critical and academic contexts — meaning what literary critics should do, how literature should be taught in universities, how it should be read, and which texts should appear on the syllabus. As Young implies, there has been a tendency in recent years for the literary syllabus to expand, so that for many English departments, for instance, 'English' literature may now mean any literature in English, and may include literature in translation and non-literary texts.

I consider this to be a significant change, not least because there is a sense in which any innovative text may reshape one's notion of the literary and its peculiar capacities. More concretely, in places where, as I suggested in the Preface, the politicized rhetoric and iconoclasm of much contemporary criticism have succeeded in dismantling a certain canon, the curatorial aspect of critical work has resurfaced with a fresh importance. To some critics this may appear a relatively conservative and modest part of the job, but the task of pointing and returning readers (and students) to worthwhile texts is one at which criticism can claim a certain effectiveness, and of course it does this not just through focusing on one text rather than another, but through communicating how rich an experience the encounter with certain texts may be. That encounter may be analysed theoretically, as it is, in terms of the literary 'event', by Attridge in *The Singularity of Literature*,[2] or enacted through an attentive literary criticism of the sort embodied in Parry's essay here, which delves into the disorientating effects and disquieting political implications of Salih's *Season of Migration to the North*. Salih's text is reasonably well-known, but it is not part of the traditional canon, and may well be the sort of writing Young has in mind in speaking of new forms of 'authentic art'.

Yet critics who wish to shift or expand the canon may believe that certain writers have been neglected because they were women, say, or non-metropolitan, rather than because their writing inherently or invariably transgresses aesthetic norms or broaches novel topics; the syllabus, especially of recent literature, has in any case never stopped evolving; and the literary event may also be experienced on re-reading a familiar passage from Shakespeare, as Attridge does in his present essay. Thus it is not clear that there is any general point to be made about the impact of a text such as Salih's, as an example of 'postcolonial writing', on the 'aesthetic criteria of the literary'. How 'postcolonial' and 'minority' writing are to be defined is not explicit in this brief passage from Young, but if, as is often the case, it is in terms of authorial identity and/or of theme, the sorts of change described by Young may have no *particular* implications for the notion of the literary as such.

Young himself appears to hesitate on this point, in that he states that writing is now valued *as much* for its depiction of representative minority experience as for its aesthetic qualities. Even in terms of syllabus design, this would imply that aesthetic and/or literary criteria have not been abandoned, even if, for some teachers or readers, their importance has lessened. And even if their importance has lessened, it is far from clear that the criteria as such have changed, let alone been revolutionized. The *aesthetic* or literary qualities of a chosen text are not determined by that text's theme any more than by the identity or experiences of its author; and I do not think there is any way to derive a concept of the *literary*, or of 'authentic *art*', from the new forms of cultural capital to which Young alludes.

Literary and aesthetic criteria may indeed be abandoned, of course, when the more drastic change occurs whereby critics and teachers in 'literature' departments, or former literature departments, come to feel that the object of their attention need not or should not be 'literary' at all. Even this has no necessary conceptual implications for the literary object that has been left behind, but it clearly has pragmatic consequences, not least in relation to the curatorial aspect of critical activity to which I have just alluded. Moreover, the shift from 'literary' to 'cultural' studies is often associated with a debunking of literature's claims to a special status, as well as a kind of politicization of the objects and methods of study.

In view of the impetus she has provided to these same academic shifts, one of the more striking recent returns to the literary is that made by Gayatri Spivak in *Death of a Discipline*. The book marks both an old and a new direction for Spivak, or at least for Spivak the famous postcolonialist, staging a different academic persona from the one projected by her large-scale work of 1999, *A Critique of Postcolonial Reason*.[3] There Spivak remarked: 'my book charts a practitioner's progress from colonial discourse studies to transnational cultural studies' (ix−x). Not untypically, her early progress as a U.S.-based 'practitioner' actually *began* elsewhere, with a thesis, supervised by Paul de Man, on the life and poetry of W.B. Yeats, but quite frequently in more recent texts Spivak has come across as one of those postcolonial critics who are almost embarrassed to be tied to literature by training and disciplinary affiliation. To some readers it will come as a surprise, then, that Spivak's new book aims to promote 'the proper study of literature' (*Death of a Discipline*, 13).

Death of a Discipline begins by considering the history and inter-relation of area studies, cultural and postcolonial studies, and comparative literature. It is greatly concerned with academic structures and pedagogy. Important to Spivak's notion of 'the proper study of literature' is 'the skill of reading closely in the original', one she would like to see more widely practiced outside literary studies in the 'major' languages of the old European powers. Area studies and cultural studies specialists often share the comparatist's ability to read foreign languages, but they tend, Spivak claims, to treat them merely as 'field' languages or tools. The additional level of sophistication that she wishes to promote, and that she finds in comparative literature, involves 'entering into the idiom' and in that sense is not just linguistic, and not just a matter of seeking out cultural material from new sources and with new perspectives, desirable though that may be. Cultural studies, by contrast — and in the US, cultural studies seems to take on the role of pre-eminent adversary for those 'defending' the literary[4] — is castigated for being 'tied to plot summary masquerading as analysis of representation, and character analysis by a precritical model of motivation' (19).[5]

What matters most to Spivak with regard to literary specificity is the sort of response associated with it, and it is perhaps on this issue that she diverges most sharply from her 'cultural studies' self and from the remarks I quoted from Young. Young's phrase about the 'depiction of representative minority experience' seems to suggest that the contemporary reader (/student) will be turning to the text for a view of and information about a 'minority' culture (most often, presumably, someone else's) and that the text's 'depiction' of experience will be taken to be reliable and authoritative; and this in turn may suggest that the author has a responsibility to write reliably in this way. I will return in due course to the shortcomings of this approach. But in defence of the 'information retrieval' model of reading, one might point out that there is a sense in which there is indeed a lot of 'information' in nearly all novels (if not in all literature). This may include information about the places and times in which fictional action is set. Partly for this reason, many of our everyday assumptions hold good, with regard to both unspoken, 'infra-informational' aspects of the fictional world (for instance, the assumed effects of gravity) and aspects of that world that have functional significance (for instance, skin colour). To make sense of a text and to get something out of it, readers generally need to assume that there are all sorts of continuities between fictional worlds and the world they inhabit. As Thomas Pavel puts it, 'Beyond particular objects [individuals, actions...], writers of fiction do not invent very much, since *properties* and *abstract notions* found in fiction are virtually always part of the actual world.' It is on this basis, he goes on, that 'works of fiction, just like historical studies', function as '*inferential projects* that entice the reader to link particular events narrated about particular objects to properties and abstract notions at various levels of generality.'[6] Texts may encourage or complicate this process by creating and playing on specific continuities with their own contexts, but they may also, in many instances, simply produce non-thematized, seemingly unselfconscious continuities at various levels, and reproduce sense-making mechanisms with which the reader is already familiar. In this sense, ultimately prejudicial discourse on 'racial' difference, for example, including fleeting discursive uses of 'race' as an identifying mark, may function identically inside and outside the literary text.[7]

This sort of assumption about reception lies behind many ideological criticisms of literary texts, in that it apparently gives ideological critics a basis on which to ignore the literary 'framing' of ideological discourse as irrelevant to their concerns. Chinua Achebe, for instance, argued famously that the 'layers of insulation' between Conrad and the 'moral universe' of *Heart of Darkness* (which takes the form of a story within a story, each with its own idiosyncratic narrator) had no bearing on his claims concerning the work's racism, as Conrad had failed to provide readers with 'an alternative frame of reference'.[8] This dismissal of the story's own 'frame of reference' stems in part, I suppose, from the feeling that issues such as sexism or racism and cultural difference are primarily extra-literary and have a continuing political urgency, by the standards of which literary-critical work of a traditional sort, including attention to the complexities of narrative perspective, may appear apolitical and trivial. Achebe's gesture was also more specifically iconoclastic, in that it was directed at a canonical author and via him at a certain idea of the literary and of literary tradition, particularly the idea that literature is apolitical and timeless. One of the worries for a critic such as Achebe is that such notions may actually increase rather than lessen the influence of political discourses traversing the literary space, in that readers who imagine that space to be apolitical and timeless may lower their critical defences, and/or may feel that their particular worldview has been endorsed as natural and universal by the text.

At this point we are still concerned with pedagogy and reception, but the model of reading has shifted. The model brought into play by Achebe's critique is still characterized by a certain indistinction between fiction or the literary and the real, but his focus is more on what I called 'everyday assumptions' than on 'information-retrieval', since he is most worried about readers who are quietly absorbing imperialist attitudes while imagining themselves to be concerned with higher matters. The most important aspect of this shift is that Achebe's model does not underpin his own reading (or 'reading', in the sense of critical interpretation) of the text, and indeed is quite the opposite of a 'model' in the positive sense. Rather, a certain mode of reading is attributed to other, less alert, less well-informed readers.

It would be easy to make this critical move sound reprehensible (elitist, prejudiced), but the authority of critics who believe that their voice is worth hearing, and of teachers who believe that textual interpretation can be taught, must rest on the idea that some people read better than others. Moreover, critics, such as Achebe here, whose ultimate concern is with the political impact of literary texts, have no alternative but to seek information on, and to speculate on, reading and reception. One often reads critics' claims about a text's subversive qualities (or the opposite) but the political grounding of such claims is unclear until the question is addressed of *whose* attitudes the text subverts, or once subverted. Most ideological theories of literature, I would argue, are reception theories, although they do not always recognize themselves as such, or offer any explicit theory of reception.

By the same token, I would accept that in some cases, critical moves of Achebe's sort may be legitimate, both in trying to imagine how other readers have reacted to a given text, and in consequently discounting as ideologically irrelevant certain facets of that text. Yet in the case of *Heart of Darkness*, I do not believe Achebe's approach is well founded, for reasons linked with that text in particular and also with the disposition of the literary text as such. Here I will not rehearse the argument about *Heart of Darkness* itself, but will use this well-known example to raise more general issues. Clearly, in the case of *Heart of Darkness* the way the text has been read has varied greatly. Achebe's attack on the text is not just an example of variation from the norm as he perceived it, but itself remains well-known because of its impact on the subsequent history of reception, particularly its treatment by literary critics. Achebe's own account of the text's reception is too homogenized, because insufficiently historicized: the text's engagement with 'colonial discourse' and racism is much more extensive and concrete than he allows, containing specific details, concerning Belgian colonialism and the debates around it, that would have been recognized immediately by Conrad's first readers. In other words, the text does, or did, bring into play more than one ideological framework from its own historical context, and would have been read accordingly when perhaps it most mattered — that is, at the turn of the century, as the fate of the Congo Free State was contested. This historical point may not carry much weight for Achebe, whose main concern is the text's ongoing influence on attitudes to Africa. But at least as an object of critical and pedagogical attention, the text has now been reconnected with a particular episode in African history; and from Achebe's perspective, the text's capacity to be reconnected with that history (and so to introduce readers to important historical material with which they might otherwise have been unfamiliar) must surely be offset, so to speak, against its capacity to be disconnected from it.

One of the lessons to emerge from this example is that no single model of reading is likely to be adequate to critics' implicit or explicit speculations on the way a text has been or will be received, particularly if that text has been read for many years. This shows further that a precise mode or history of reception *cannot be inferred from the text itself.* To look at it from the other side, the text alone cannot impose a particular mode of reading on the reader or critic: *Heart of Darkness* could not force Achebe to read it 'literarily' in the sense of taking account of the complex framing of its historical material, any more that it could force him to recognize the extent of its engagement with that material, or to consider the possible reasons for, or benefits of, leaving much of that engagement implicit.

I stated earlier that 'prejudicial discourse on "racial" difference may function identically inside and outside the literary text', and suggested that this idea was close to Achebe's anxiety and argument. In some instances, it may well make no difference whether such discourse is inside or outside the literary text. Yet in other instances, the way that discourse functions may alter crucially once it enters literary space. This argument is again, on one level, an historical one: if, in order to assess a literary text's politics, one wishes — or, as I am arguing, *needs* — to understand how it has been read, so as to consider its political *impact*, one needs to understand the shape and weight of ideas of the literary for particular readers. Even when readers have turned to literary texts for information, their attitude to them must have been influenced to some degree by their idea of the literary, an idea communicated to them through education, literary criticism, and literature itself. All reading of literature, as literary theorists have always insisted, is literary-theoretical in that sense.

In the light of the earlier points about 'inference' and the extent of the *identity* between, or of, fiction and the world — points that would appear to cover a wide range of texts and periods — this argument may itself seem a highly 'theoretical' one. I would concede this, in the sense that I am being forced to generalize about 'literary texts' as well as readers, and would view my arguments as more pertinent, and more worthwhile, in relation to some texts than others. (The question of the curatorial aspect of critical work, and the pertinence to it of the aesthetic criteria of the literary, arises again here.) But I would also argue, in quite general terms, that the relationship readers establish with literary texts is indeed highly conventionalized, and involves complex forms of self-consciousness and awareness of the norms of literary representation. The play of readerly 'identification', for instance, may appear at first sight to involve some sort of profound confusion of representation and the real, in that the reader feels 'involved', may cry real tears, and so on. It may appear, then, that readers are apt to lose all self-consciousness and critical distance, in ways that make it all the more likely they will imbibe unthinkingly any ideological toxins swilling around the text, as Achebe appears to fear. Yet readers' willingness to expose themselves to texts that will make them cry, or scare them, shows that this response also involves some fundamental form of uninvolvement, non–identification, and self-consciousness, as does the fact that the emotions aroused in this way rarely persist in the way that emotions prompted by (other) personal experiences do.

The argument I have just made, to summarize, is that no critic working with literature can abandon the idea of the literary without risking particular forms of essentialism and ahistoricism: ideas of the literary needs to be taken into account even by those critics who are concerned only with the ideological work that literature may do or has done, or with literature's ability to communicate 'experience', if only because ideas of the literary have formed an integral part of the shifting conventions of authorship and reception. One cannot gain an accurate sense of the ideological impact of a literary text without some grasp of the history of literature and literary reception as such.

Even working with an adequate model of literary reception, however, one needs, if one's ultimate concern is, say, racism, to justify pursuing that topic in relation to literature. One justification might be 'quantitative', that is to say, an argument that literature had played an important or even pre-eminent role in the transmission of racial ideologies. I am sceptical about the possibility of sustaining that argument, historically or even theoretically, but cannot pursue that question here. The justification I will consider further is 'qualitative', which means going beyond the question of critics' need for an histor-ical sense of literary specificity to address again the issue of literary specificity itself. This question too, I would argue, is of interest to any critic dealing with literary texts at all. If a 'quantitative' argument fails or cannot be supported, it is hard to see how one can justify a literary approach to a primarily non-literary issue unless literature has something particular to 'say' about racism, or offers something other than the information and analyses one could find in a politics or history textbook.

That 'something', on which I will make just a few remarks in the rest of this essay, is an issue for all of the contributors to this collection, and of much other recent work. For example, Parry presents *Season of Migration to the North* as raising difficult questions about 'the interpenetration of cognitive and aesthetic dimensions' (see below, 72), while the possibility of reconfiguring the relations between bodies and language, and language and the (currently) unthinkable, is raised by Rancière, Jarvis and Badiou. Thereby they also cast light on a long and deep-rooted history of suspicion of literature and art, and one that may lie behind or within some of the more recent academic trends to which I have alluded.[9] My own understanding of this issue has been strongly influenced by Derrida, with whose thought Attridge, among the present contributors, is most closely engaged.

Attridge's *The Singularity of Literature* concludes, drawing on Derrida, that 'the literary occupies, in the practices and understandings of Western culture, the place of the other' (137). Spivak too turns to Derrida at this point, and in *Death of a Discipline* discusses literature's value in terms of *poiesis* and *teleopoiesis*, borrowing the latter term from Derrida's *Politiques de l'amitié*.[10] *Poiesis* is glossed by Spivak as an 'imaginative making', associated with a far-reaching experience of cultural dis- or re-orientation, and she wishes to 'reclaim the role of teaching literature as training the imagination—the great inbuilt instrument of othering' (13). If I understand Spivak correctly, she uses the prefix 'teleo-' to mark a distance between, on the one hand, a certain self-conscious, future-oriented act of imagination, and, on the other, a hubristic 'mapmaking' (31). Her point, I think, is that the imaginative process should serve less to bring home the unfamiliar than to allow one to project oneself into a radically 'other' space while acknowledging that it remains partially but intractably unknowable.[11]

Such notions of an encounter with alterity, modelled and/or facilitated in a specific way by the literary text and a corresponding mode of literary reading, are at a considerable distance from the search, as described by Young, for 'representative minority experience'. As I have already implied, there are texts for which it would be hard to claim the profound transports of 'teleopoiesis', but this is not determined by the text's theme; rather, it would seem to be a matter of the text's 'literary' qualities, which in some sense force the reader to 'enter the idiom' in Spivak's sense. Through the example of *Heart of Darkness* I stressed that no text can fully determine its own reception, and that the history of reception has its own momentum, whose direction most texts can hope to influence only minimally. Nevertheless, certain texts work to render their own 'literariness' — or, one might say, their own 'alterity' — unmistakable. In practice the issue may be partly generic: most poetry, for instance, cannot easily be mistaken for anything else, by virtue of its printed form and/or its internal structure, and most poems make it even harder than does *Heart of Darkness* to ignore this specificity or to dissociate content from form. This could also be expressed in terms of poetry's particular ability to establish itself as unparaphrasable, an issue addressed by Russell's essay in terms of the poetic functions of repetition and tautology. Yet in principle (as Russell suggests) this principle extends to the literary as such, an argument pursued in a radical and general fashion by Bessière in his analysis of the unavoidable facticity of the literary work. By definition, for Bessière, or by its nature, the literary text imposes itself as such.

Young's remarks on the recent downplaying of texts' aesthetic qualities might be taken to imply, as might Achebe's, that any striving towards literary/formal specificity, and perhaps towards aesthetic distinction, and the critical practices tracking and promoting this endeavour, should be seen as distancing the text not just from information but from politics. This issue, raised implicitly by Spivak, is of course the subject of longstanding and often polarized debate. One version of literary politics may be emblematized by the Sartre of *Qu'est-ce que la littérature?*, an essay that remains an important reference point, especially in the French-speaking world.[12] Sartre's long shadow is most evident in Badiou's title (to which I will return shortly), but also apparent in Rancière's essay, for instance in his allusions to Sartre's treatment of Flaubert, and is perhaps fleetingly visible in Bessière's remark that 'every literary narrative represents a narrative exchange without pragmatic commitment (*sans engagement pragmatique*)' (see below, 49). And in an email, the other French-language contributor, Djebar, described her contribution as 'un court texte, en forme de poème, du genre "qu'est-ce qu'écrire"'. ('Qu'est-ce qu'écrire?' or 'What is writing?', as Djebar undoubtedly knows, is the title of the first section of Sartre's book.) The Sartre of *Qu'est-ce que la littérature?* felt, of course, that poetry as a genre was not a suitable vehicle for political commitment (*engagement*) as he prescribed it, and he was highly critical of Flaubert, a writer of 'poetic' prose with no apparent political aims.[13]

Another version of literary politics may be found in the subsequent work of the *Tel Quel* group and its associates, who in some respects can be seen as having taken up the torch of the historic avant-garde through their commitment to the subversive potential of a certain practice of literary textuality. The *Tel Quel* critics thus tended to favour Flaubert over Balzac, say, and to situate the former as one of the earlier representatives of their own favoured subcanon, whose most prominent members included Mallarmé and Blanchot. In some ways Young appears closer to the Sartrean pole, not least because his argument needs us to take seriously the notion of 'authentic art' in his second sentence (although one might ask if that is any less an 'outdated category of elitist institutions' than is the idea of the literary), and in that his approach seems to imply a preference for readily identifiable political themes. In other respects, however, his comments have a more avant-gardist tone, notably in their conjoining of political and aesthetic vocabulary and their invocation of 'elitist institutions'. One of the ironies of Young's position is that it draws some of its energy from the very literary/aesthetic tradition that it may appear to be leaving behind: if the idea of a 'revolution' in aesthetic criteria of the literary seems inspiring, the inspiration has undoubtedly come not just from a political tradition, but from a literary and aesthetic tradition too.[14]

In the literary tradition promoted by *Tel Quel*, among others, the texts that are seen to be the most 'revolutionary' — the most radical, the most profound, and also the 'most political' — distinguish themselves, and may be grouped together, in terms of qualities that cannot but be labelled literary or aesthetic, and certainly not in terms of any explicit politics. Those texts are sometimes presented as the very paradigm of modern literature.[15] Derrida, among others, sometimes uses 'literature' to allude specifically to such texts, and it is certainly this tradition (among other things) that Derrida has in mind when he states: 'there are perhaps forms of thought that think more than does that thought called philosophy (*il y a peut-être des pensées plus pensantes que cette pensée qu'on appelle philosophie*)'.[16] This issue is raised too by Badiou's title, 'Qu'est-ce que la littérature pense?':[17] in each case the implication is that literary 'thought' or literature's particular capabilities cannot be captured in the terms of Sartrean *engagement*, and reach their highest form in texts oblivious or even hostile to it.

From this perspective, it appears not only that some 'literary' texts are more literary than others — Badiou's seemingly general question about literary thinking is answered through a consideration of 'literature that thinks (*la littérature qui pense*)', implying that not all 'literature' does (see below, 36) — but also that the 'most literary' texts are perhaps the most subversive too, in a sense precisely because less political in an obvious sense. But the 'perhaps' in that last sentence must, I think, be a permanent aspect of this line of thought, and corresponds to Derrida's 'perhaps' when he says 'there are perhaps forms of thought that think more than does that thought called philosophy': in so far as this literary 'thinking' is held genuinely to be irreducible to political thought and untranslatable into any other set of representational conventions, it must remain indescribable in some important sense, merely gestured towards by the sort of criticism (by Derrida himself, say, or by Blanchot) that itself tends towards a literary idiom. It must thus remain indeterminate in its effects, and in this sense must run the risk of inconsequentiality. In the present collection, Rancière touches on this issue when he writes of 'the risk of eventually rendering the music of the Idea indistinguishable from the prose of the world' (a phrase that resonates alongside Jarvis's consideration of 'musical thinking'), and he remarks that 'it seems doubtful that literature might ever be able to offer the guarantee of goodwill sometimes demanded of it: namely of capturing worldly experience in such a way as to help configure a shared universe of political debate, judgement and action' (see below, 101).

This does not imply that those interested in and sympathetic to enquiries into the specificity of literary work need work always and only at this level of abstraction, or dedicate themselves exclusively to the texts that are 'most literary' in these terms or to their most literary aspects, still less that they must eschew texts that appear to have political aims. To read *Heart of Darkness*, a deeply political text, 'literarily', does not mean focusing only on its formal literary characteristics; indeed, I think that project is completely inconceivable. Derrida captures this well when he writes: 'There is no literature without a *suspended* relation to meaning and reference (...) *Suspended* means *suspense*, but also *dependence*, condition, conditionality', or when he remarks elsewhere: 'literature (...) always is, it says, it does something else, something other than itself, and it itself moreover is only that, something other than itself.'[18] The experience of the literary text is simultaneously an experience of the non-literary, in practice; it is mixed and multi-faceted, engaging on one level with issues of reference (history, one might say, or experience), and on another level with those aspects of the text that defer or frustrate reference. The nature of the 'suspension' of reference is such, however, that these levels are inextricable: even as it appears to offer 'information' of one sort or another, the literary text cannot itself ever indicate reliably which 'information' within it is truthful or 'representative' or, for that matter, is drawn from the author's own experience. This inextricability also means that although, in one sense, as I suggested just now, some texts are 'more literary' than others, in another sense, 'degrees' of literariness are immeasurable. A text's (apparent) claims to referentiality are suspended, in Derrida's terms, or they are not; and this occurs not within the text but in the dialectic between text and reader, a dialectic shaped by the idea of the literary or what Derrida calls the 'institution' of literature.

Many of the arguments I have discussed in this essay, and many of the other contributions to this collection, concern the relation between literature and politics, and it will have been apparent that I, like others, am drawn to the argument that the 'most literary' texts are the 'most political'. But I am not fully convinced by it, and to 'defend' the literary in such terms is to risk continuing to subordinate it to the political (or to a conventional notion of the political) in a way that again may render it ultimately indefensible, if to do so means accepting tacitly that 'distance' from the political is something that always needs to be justified politically. If one pursues the point about literary indeterminacy rigorously (bearing in mind, once again, Derrida's 'perhaps'), I am not sure that such a justification can be firmly established; the distance is irreducible, and indissociable from the literary as such, which thus needs to be defended in its 'own terms', in some sense.[19]

This leads me back to Young's remarks on how the literary 'is now valued', and to the final contribution to this volume, Djebar's poem. Djebar's work in general is unmistakably engaged with politics and history, in ways that mean many of her readers value her writing for its representation of 'minority' experience, to echo Young's comments, and for the kind of 'voice' it lends Algerian/Muslim women. But her writing is also distinguished by its qualities of uncertainty and self-questioning, its indirection and occasional opacity, its blending and confusion of registers, and the other varied ways in which it attempts to position itself in that literary space, described by Derrida and others, where no interpretation is definitive and no connexion between the text and the author unequivocally drawn. That space is one to which 'minority' authors have had particular trouble gaining access, of course. But there is no doubt that some writers, including some 'postcolonial' writers such as Djebar, value precisely that indeterminacy or distancing that I, following Derrida, have used to characterize the literary.

If the literary, conceived in such terms, is seen as inherently elitist and conservative, the political critic may wonder why someone like Djebar, as an undeniably political writer, wants anything to do with it. One answer may be, of course, that she happens, irrespective of her politics, to be drawn precisely to its aesthetic aspects; and one of the most difficult issues to address in the current critical climate is the extent to which the value of some literary texts, or aspects of all literary texts — and perhaps, by the same token, of some academic work — may ultimately be something apolitical or non-political. But another answer may be that Djebar (which is to say, the individual for whom Assia Djebar is a pen-name) is drawn to the literary precisely because of her own experiences, including her own relationship to political discourse. It may thus be a matter of self-protection and self-disguise: she has complained before about censorious responses to her work by 'Zhdanovist' critics unhappy with her writing's relation to anti-colonial nationalism;[20] and she has the experiences of a 'member' of an oppressed 'minority' with regard to the prejudicial mechanism that treats every member of that minority as its representative at every point, not least when that individual is a writer. But to reiterate my earlier point, her literary texts themselves, even though they may prompt these speculations, cannot, by definition, unequivocally confirm or reject them. My own view of Djebar's writing is that it is at its most interesting when most evidently 'mixed', in prose, in its engagements with historiography and autobiography; but, for reasons at which I have already hinted, a poem may well have been the most appropriate form in which to respond to, and resist, the request to state her views on the literary; and 'Ecrire'/'Writing', which appears to dwell precisely on the reasons why anyone writes (or why she writes), and on what literary writing may be, joins other works of Djebar's in considering writing both as a means of capturing and channelling some project of 'liberty', and as an exercise in interiority, even silence, and as a physical and aesthetic experience that exceeds conscious control.

The critic has particular responsibilities, I believe, towards a writer such as Djebar, and to the literary freedom that she has sought to win for herself. It appears from Djebar's literary texts themselves, finally, among many others, that literary writing should be allowed, and valued for, the peculiar and partial kind of freedom it offers the writer from both her self and the norms of representation and interpretation, and which is unthinkable without a notion of the literary as such. The critic or theorist, even in a field such as postcolonial studies, needs to go beyond the search for depictions of representative minority experience, if she or he wishes to deal with the literary at all, to treat texts in their specificity (and so to avoid falling into incoherence), and to respond adequately to the work of new and old writers alike. Derrida remarks that 'the "best" reading would consist in *giving oneself up* to the most idiomatic aspects of the work while also *taking account* of the historical context, of what is *shared* (in the sense of both participation and division, of continuity and the cut of separation), of what belongs to genre and type (. . .) and any work is singular in that it speaks singularly of both singularity and generality'.[21] This approach allows the critic to recognize, where appropriate, the profoundly and extensively political dimension of many literary texts without reducing the texts to that dimension, and so without losing any ultimate justification for focusing on or passing via the literary text; and it implies a certain openness to the text's work (and to the eventuality of 'teleopoiesis', one might say), as well as a determination to *do justice* to the text. All the essays in this collection, I believe, lend support to the idea that criticism may both embody and promote 'justice' of this order, and has a duty to do so, at a theoretical level and/or as an inextricable part of the process of interpretation.

NICHOLAS HARRISON

NOTES

Abbreviated references will be given for publications listed in the Preface.

1 Robert Young, 'Ideologies of the Postcolonial', Editorial in *Interventions* 1:1 (1998/9), 4–8.
2 London and New York, Routledge, 2004.
3 *A Critique of Postcolonial Reason: Toward a History of the Vanishing Present* (Cambridge and London, Harvard University Press, 1999).
4 For a provocative critique of assumptions in cultural studies about literary culture's elitism and other failings, see John Brenkman, 'Extreme criticism'. This excellent essay, which argues that 'The social and the aesthetic problematic of literature (. . .) meet in the form of literature itself', is also critical of most formulations of 'the literary'. In Judith Butler et al, *What's left of theory*, 114–36.

5   In her Acknowledgements, written two years after the lectures of May 2000 on which the book is based, Spivak states that Comparative Literature in the United States underwent a sea change in the intervening period, such that her text should be read as the discipline's 'last gasp' (xii), and it is to the death of comparative literature that her title alludes. These remarks prompted an acid response from her French reviewer, Didier Coste, on the literary theory website *Fabula*. Coste noted that, according to Spivak, 'Things change at great speed in Comparative Literature in the USA — as they did, for example, between 2000 and 2002 (the cause of the disruption, it goes without saying, being the 11th of September). From a less short-sighted, less ahistorical point of view, it would be just as striking that almost nothing has changed in the discipline in France for decades' ('Votum Mortis', www.fabula.org/cgi-bin/imprimer.pl?doc=/revue/cr.449.php, 27.01.04). I am not convinced that things are so static in France, but Spivak's engagement with the academic landscape in which she works certainly seems characteristic of that landscape, not least because of her heightened sense of disciplinary development and direction (albeit, in this case, towards death): only in that context, I suspect, could such a gulf of retrospection open up within two years.

6   Pavel, review of Dorrit Cohn, *The Distinction of Fiction* (Baltimore, John Hopkins University Press, 1998), *Comparative Literature* 53:1 (Winter 2001), 83–5: 84.

7   Here and in my observations on *Heart of Darkness*, I am summarizing arguments that I have made at greater length in *Postcolonial Criticism: History, Theory and the Work of Fiction* (Cambridge, Polity, 2003).

8   'An image of Africa: Racism in Conrad's *Heart of Darkness*', *Hopes and Impediments: Selected Essays, 1965–1987* (Oxford, Heinemann, 1988), 1–13: 7.

9   This issue is also central to Rancière's fascinating recent book, *Malaise dans l'esthétique* (Paris, Galilée, 2004).

10 Paris, Galilée, 1994; *Politics of Friendship*, translated by George Collins (London, Verso, 1997).

11 Spivak's example of 'a failure of teleopoiesis' in the field of international feminism helps clarify things: 'We saw this (...) as Afghan women became the flavor of the day in November 2001. "They are dating and shopping," crooned Diane Sawyer' (*Death of a Discipline*, 50).

12 Paris, Gallimard, 1948; *What is Literature?* translated by Bernard Frechtman (London, Methuen, 1950).

13 Sartre's own position changed drastically, to the point where he considered Flaubert a 'committed' writer, but *Qu'est-ce que la littérature?* remains his most influential statement of the relations between literature and politics. Christina Howells provides an excellent account of Sartre's literary theory in Chapter 6 of *Sartre: The Necessity of Freedom* (Cambridge, Cambridge University Press, 1988).

14 This also means, again, a literary-theoretical tradition that has valorized aesthetic innovation and revolution. There are innumerable examples; from the *Tel Quel* group, Kristeva's La *Révolution du langage poétique. L'Avant-garde à la fin du XIXe siècle: Lautréamont et Mallarmé* (Paris, Seuil, 1974; English translation 1984) is one of the more influential.

15 Of recent work, Rancière's *La Parole muette: Essai sur les contradictions de la littérature* (Paris, Hachette, 1998) is among the most important here. On the roots of this paradigm in German romanticism, see too the influential text by Lacoue-Labarthe and Nancy, *L'Absolu littéraire: Théorie de la littérature du romantisme allemand* (Paris, Seuil, 1978); *The Literary Absolute* (Albany, SUNY Press, 1988).

16 Cited by Timothy Clark in his fine book *Derrida, Heidegger, Blanchot: Sources of Derrida's notion and practice of literature* (Cambridge University Press, 1992), 19.

17 A closely comparably issue is central to Jarvis's essay on 'Musical thinking' in the current collection, though it is discussed with reference to prosody and the 'musical' aspects of language in general, and in relation to different authors.

18 *Acts of Literature,* 48; *Passions,* 94. One may compare Bessière's concluding remark, 'The autonomous literary work is heterogeneous' (see below, 55).

19 One of the arguments of Lacoue-Labarthe and Nancy in *The Literary Absolute* is that the terms in which literature is currently thought are not 'its own' but emerge from a Romantic philosophical tradition. Their point is not, however, to subordinate literature to philosophy, and I think their analysis is compatible with my own arguments about the literary as such and about the insubordination, so to speak, of the literary to politics.

20 See Djebar's collection of essays, *Ces voix qui m'assiègent ... en marge de ma francophonie* (Paris, Albin Michel, 1999) — for example pages 18 and 87. See too Derrida's passing reference to Zhdanovism, *Acts of Literature,* 38.

21 *Acts of Literature,* 68. The relation between singularity and generality is an important one for Attridge, and also, in a different way, for Steven Knapp, whose *Literary Interest* sees a correlation between literature's characteristic relation of the particular to the general and the structure of human agency as such.

Performing Metaphors: The Singularity of Literary Figuration

I

This essay is an extension and elaboration of one aspect of an argument I presented very briefly in *The Singularity of Literature*.[1] That book was an attempt to develop a vocabulary by means of which to discuss the distinctiveness of literature as a cultural practice, responding to the work of a number of writers, critics, and philosophers, the most important of whom was Jacques Derrida.[2] In the interest of clarity and brevity I won't try in what follows to identify all the sources of my thinking, or the positions against which my own has emerged over many years; most of my debts will, in any case, be evident. I begin with a sketch of the central argument of the book, before going on to the more particular issue I want to discuss.

The proposal at the heart of *The Singularity of Literature* is that the *work of art* — a phrase I would like to be taken in two senses — as a feature of Western culture (indeed, as one of the ways in which that culture has for a long time defined itself) can be usefully understood by means of a trinity of terms, each of which is implicated in the other two: *alterity*, *invention*, and *singularity*. Clearly, each of these terms requires further specification, as they are used in many different ways in aesthetic and philosophical discourses. All I have space for here is the barest summary, and I'll have to leave a number of questions unaddressed.

Alterity (or *otherness*) refers to the work of art's challenge to existing frameworks of knowledge, feeling, and behaviour. This is not a matter of simply *opposing* accepted norms, since opposition occurs within a shared horizon; rather, it is the introduction into the known of that which it excludes in constituting itself as the known. (When I say 'known', I'm letting the word do duty for a much wider array of habits, expectations, prejudices, beliefs, and traditions than it normally suggests.) Because the known *depends* on this exclusion, the introduction of that which is excluded — we can call it 'the other' if we like — requires a shift in the norms and habits on which we normally rely for our dealings with the inner and outer worlds we inhabit.

Although novelty has been more valued in certain periods than in others, the artists we regard as significant have always sought to bring into being works that in some way go beyond the familiar — even if they do so only by presenting the familiar in a slightly unfamiliar light. The power of the work of art lies in the shifting of habitual ways of thinking and feeling that enables both the artist and the respondent (using this rather inadequate word to cover the reader, the viewer, and the listener) to acknowledge alterity. What is peculiar about works of art, however, in contrast to other irruptions of alterity into the cultural field (we might think of philosophical arguments, scientific discoveries, mechanical inventions), is that they can *sustain* their alterity across time, both the time of generations and the time from one reading, viewing, or listening to another.

The coming-into-being of the work of art is, I argue, both an *act* and an *event*; it is something the artist *does* (or a number of artists *do* in a collaborative process) and something that *happens to* the artist (or artists). The name I give to this act-event is (and here is the second item in my trinity) *invention*, a handy term since it refers also to the product of the act-event. And it brings together the artist who creates the work and the person who experiences it: in responding to a painting or a poem as an invention, in other words, I am responding both to the object and to the act-event that produced it (even if I know nothing, in historical or biographical terms, about that act-event). As Blanchot puts it, the reader 'partakes of the work as the unfolding of something in the making'.[3] It is for this reason that the alterity of the artwork does not, in some cases at least, disappear as the culture learns to accommodate itself to it. Unlike the mechanical invention, which effects a change and then ceases to be surprising, the artwork can remain inventive, never wholly assimilated — or it can become inventive in new ways as the culture alters. The inventiveness to which we respond is unlikely to be identical with what a contemporary of the artist would have regarded as its inventiveness; in fact, it is the work's openness to new contexts that enables its inventiveness to persist. (By contrast, the work's *originality* is a historical fact about it, always open to reassessment as we gain more information, that may or may not be part of our enjoyment of it.)

Invention, as Derrida puts it, is always *the invention of the other* (and you'll notice how the ambiguity of that phrase encapsulates the doubleness of the act-event). And what is invented is always — this is the third of the three interrelated terms — *singular*. That is, the alterity of a work of art is not some quality or property that may be present to a greater or lesser degree; it is indissociable from the work's identity as a recognisable work (through all its mutations). The long-held view that the work of art is, or should be, *unique* is a reflection of this aspect, although to stress uniqueness is to imply that the work has an unchanging and circumscribed core, whereas singularity, in the sense in which I am using it, depends on openness to change and porousness in new contexts.

How, then, do we respond to the work of art *as* a work of art, and not as any of the large number of other things that it may also be (a historical document, a biographical utterance, a psychological betrayal, a social marker, a political intervention, etc.)? Clearly, we respond to its inventiveness, alterity and singularity as a challenge of some sort to our expectations and habits. But this must mean more than enumerating its qualities or analysing its elements: we have to do justice to it as an event, and to the eventness of that event. It must happen anew in our response, each time we read it. Putting it in a different metaphoric register, we must *perform* it; or more accurately, and preserving the undecidability between act and event, when we read a literary work as a literary work *we find ourselves performing it*. (I'm willing to leave the ambiguity of that phrase unresolved too.)

This is the part of my argument to which I would like to devote a little more attention. Performance, like most of the terms I am using, has a multiplicity of meanings, but I hope my use of it will be clear. In performing the work of art (which may be a sculpture I am looking at or a piece of music I am listening to) I am making it happen, as a singular, inventive other impinging on my culturally and historically specific situation as a subject. In doing so, what I am making happen is the work's *own* singular performance — of the effects of light, say, of the dynamics of narrative, of the emotive possibilities of sound, and so on. I am, if you like, living through its performance, not simply observing it.

To make this discussion more precise, I need to limit myself to literature; there are too many different kinds of performance involved in the different art forms for a general account to get us very far. A work of literature can perform — or stage, or enact — anything that language can do. By using these theatrical terms, I mean to bring out the element of self-distancing that is involved, what Derrida calls the *suspension* of the normal properties of language:[4] the language of a literary work may function in exactly the same way as the language of daily life, *except* that as long as we are reading it as literary language its operations are on show, its powers operative yet not quite closed down onto a non-linguistic world. Thus, to take an example, one of language's most useful properties is referentiality, its capacity to send the hearer or reader to something outside itself. The literary work *stages* referentiality, so that while it continues to propel the hearer or reader in this manner it simultaneously interrupts the process by making the very process of referral part of the point: we are affected not just by what is being referred to but by the power of language to refer, and of *this* language to refer in *this* way.

The category of literature thus differs from the category of *fiction*, the distinguishing feature of which is that the objects and events referred to are imaginary.[5] The literary work may refer to real as well as to imaginary events; it is the *staging* of referentiality that marks it as literary — in a literary reading, that is. It is perfectly possible for a work of history to be open to (and to yield fruitfully to) a literary reading. It is perfectly possible to read a single work in more than one manner at once; in fact, it is probably impossible not to. If I enjoy E. P. Thompson's *Making of the English Working Class* as literature, this does not mean I cease to enjoy it, and learn from it, as history.

Let me be clear, though. My argument is *not* that we become necessarily conscious of the process of referring in reading a literary work: that is something we are likely to experience only occasionally, predominantly in modernist or postmodern texts. It is that the very process itself works differently, because we are reading for the event, not for the outcome. We take pleasure in the events of referring, and in the power of language thus exemplified — the power to bring before us in an instant the lushness of a garden or the gait of a tramp or the pain of a bee-sting. Description, to take a slightly different category, is not itself a literary device — it functions in many kinds of language to convey information, and once the information is conveyed its job is done; the reader of a novel, however, may well enjoy the process of describing that goes on in it, the staging of what we might call *descriptivity* in all its potency (and may want to read it again to re-experience the enjoyment). Something similar may be said of the *themes* we detect in literary works: the discovery of a theme is not peculiar to the reading of literature, but to be taken through the experience of thematizing is. Literary works don't offer knowledge, but they may stage the knowability — or the unknowability — of the world by staging the processes whereby knowledge is articulated, or whereby its articulation is resisted. Nor do they offer moral guidance, read as literature; however, language's power to evoke guilt, to crystallize ethical goals, to convey the difficulty of choice, is something many literary works enact.

Any linguistic process or capability can be staged in literature: there is nothing distinctively literary about using language to cajole, promise, frighten, endear, arouse, or anger, but the literary comes to the fore when we experience these speech acts as linguistic events. Even communication, so basic to the functions of language, is not central to literature. However, it is not a matter, as Roman Jakobson argued in a well-known essay,[6] of communication becoming displaced from its centrality by a different function when language is used in a literary way; rather, we experience the communicativeness of language *while it is communicating*, and it is this that displaces the communicative function from its dominant position.

★ ★ ★

I want to take as an example for further exploration a feature of language use often held to be highly characteristic of literature: metaphor.[7] It might seem that in metaphor we have a literary property that is not staged or performed, but that simply occurs. When used in works not conventionally classified as literature, we are often told, those works are drawing on a literary device. I want to argue, however, that when metaphors are used *without* being staged, *without* the slight sense of self-distance I've been talking about, they are not functioning in a literary way, and it makes no sense to call them literary devices.

It will help to look at a couple of passages that employ metaphorical figuration. Here is Hume, in *A Treatise of Human Nature*, on the challenge of scepticism to reason:

Reason first appears in possession of the throne, prescribing laws, and imposing maxims, with an absolute sway and authority. Her enemy, therefore, is obliged to take shelter under her protection, and by making use of rational arguments to prove the fallaciousness and imbecility of reason, produces, in a manner, a patent under her hand and seal.[8]

Now in the terms of my own argument it would be possible to say that, for a moment, Hume invites us to read his philosophical prose as literature (while not ceasing to read it as philosophy). This would mean enjoying not just the clarity of the argumentation—a *philosophical* pleasure—but the exhibition of language's power to represent such intangible entities as reason and scepticism in the guise of concrete images through the use of metaphor. And perhaps a certain kind of reader would do just that, with perfect legitimacy; it is not a question of texts having inherent properties that require them to be read in certain ways, but of how they may be read and how they respond to different kinds of reading. It seems more likely, however, that the reader working her way through *A Treatise of Human Nature* will respond only to the argument and will treat the metaphor in a purely instrumental way, as adding to the perspicuity of Hume's own reasoning at this moment when he is questioning the operations of reason. Having got the point, she can move on to the next stage of the argument.

Here, by contrast, is the first stanza of Robert Graves's 'The Dangerous Gift':

> Were I to cut my hand
>   On that sharp knife you gave me
>   (That dangerous knife, your beauty),
> I should know what to do:
>   Bandage the wound myself
> And hide the blood from you.[9]

Here, as in the passage by Hume, the metaphor invites us to understand more clearly an intangible quality, in this case a kind of beauty, by giving it a concrete form: but what makes this happen *as literature* is its invitation to participate in the unfolding of the metaphor itself, its staging of the potency of metaphoricity — and, of course, the inventiveness with which this is done, to produce a singular poem and to surprise the reader with its otherness. We take pleasure in the occurring of the metaphor as we read: the sharp knife that seems a real object in the first two lines is transformed into a way of specifying, or perhaps, more accurately, *feeling*, the perilous power of sexual beauty, but we remain aware that it is the potential of metaphoricity that is being exploited, that language is being made to exhibit its power to conflate categories and generate new compounds of meaning and emotion. (Unless, that is, the reader is not moved by the poem, and finds the lines predictable and uninventive. . .)

Another contrast that we can draw is between literary metaphor and the metaphors of the casual spoken language. The recent development of cognitive poetics has arisen in part out of the growing awareness that many of the features that have traditionally been taken as marking the literary use of language are in fact intrinsic to language use in its most common forms.[10] The employment of figurative language is one of these features. As Ronald Carter puts it in his recent study *Language and Creativity*, summarizing current work in cognitive linguistics (and echoing, perhaps unconsciously, many earlier writers, including Vico, Herder, Rousseau, and Nietzsche):

> The starting point and continuing emphasis of this research are that human language and the human mind are not *inherently* literal. In writings by cognitive linguists figurative language is seen not so much as deviant or ornamental but rather as ubiquitous in everyday language, especially spoken language. Discussions of figurative language proceed on the assumption that the fundamental roots of language are figurative.[11]

Here is one of the examples Carter has culled from the CANCODE corpus of spoken English, uttered by a retired male schoolteacher:

> The second year I had, I started off with 37 in the class I know that, of what you call dead wood the real dregs had been taken off the bottom and the cream the sour cream in our case up there had been creamed off the top and I just had this dead wood. (129)

Again, we can say that metaphor is being used in a literary manner here: that the speaker is sharing with his hearer a pleasure in the metaphorical power of language — in particular, the way in which dead metaphors can be brought to life by mixing them (*dead wood — dregs — cream*) or by developing them (*dregs — taken off the bottom*; *cream — sour cream — creamed off the top*). And certainly the reader of this speech in Carter's book will find the attraction of giving it a literary reading almost irresistible. But in the context of the give-and-take of conversation it seems more likely that the metaphorical potential of language is being used here in a purely instrumental way, to make the speaker's point as vividly as possible.

★ ★ ★

The most common account of metaphor goes something like this: we encounter, in speech or writing, a word or phrase that does not make sense if understood literally — 'This house has been far out at sea all night', for instance.[12] So we engage a different interpretative gear, which enables us to make sense of the statement through metaphor: for 'far out at sea' we understand something like 'so subject to the wind that the occupants have felt as if they were in a boat far from land, at the mercy of the elements'. Such an account makes no distinction between literary and non-literary uses of metaphor; it is as appropriate for Hume as for Graves. We can move it towards a more properly literary account if we stress the *activity* involved: the registering of an anomaly, the searching for a sense that would fit with the literal context, the experience of strangeness that is produced, the richness of the meanings made possible by the indeterminacy of the metaphor. All this is correct, but it still sounds like a recipe for the domestication of metaphor, even if we are responding to the act/event of domestication rather than to the meaning arrived at. And it rests on the somewhat wobbly foundation of the notion of *deviation*, which tends to get us into trouble because of the problem of defining the norm from which deviation occurs.

Two interesting accounts of metaphor play down the idea that our ability to interpret metaphor depends on a special linguistic ability and procedure. Dan Sperber and Deirdre Wilson present one of these in *Relevance*,[13] as part of a general theory about communication that has been immensely influential in cognitive poetics. Sperber and Wilson insist that metaphor 'requires no special interpretive abilities or procedures' (237); they regard metaphorical utterances, like all utterances, as interpretations of the speaker's *thought*. The literal utterance is only the limiting case, in which the utterance is identical to the thought; other utterances vary in some way or other from the thought they represent. The utterance can be a loose version of the thought (as when I say it is midnight when the clock I have just looked at shows 12.08), or a hyperbolic version, or a metaphoric version. This analysis has the advantage of placing metaphor in the context of a range of non-literal uses of language, and of stressing the variety within metaphoric uses themselves; the emphasis on the processing of metaphor (as part of a wider exploration of speakers' and hearers' processing activity) is also useful. However, the notion that the linguistic utterance translates a 'thought,' either literally or non-literally, assumes a binary structure that is hard to justify and that reintroduces, with all its problems, the old model of a norm from which figurative utterances deviate.[14]

A more radical account of the processing of metaphors is Donald Davidson's well-known essay, 'What Metaphors Mean'.[15] Davidson's thesis is the apparently simple one that 'metaphors mean what the words, in their most literal interpretation, mean, and nothing more' (30). This may sound like a claim that metaphors have no existence, but Davidson is in fact moving us to a domain other than that of *meaning* in which the force of metaphors is profoundly felt. As he explains, 'I depend on the distinction between what words mean and what they are used to do. I think metaphor belongs entirely to the domain of use' (31). In other words, the effectiveness of metaphoric uses of language derives from what *happens* when we hear or read them, and this is not a process of translating them back into a literal meaning or a prior 'thought' but of treating them — with whatever imaginative capacities we possess — as words with their usual meanings. The result, Davidson tells us, is that the metaphor makes us notice things that we hadn't noticed before: connections and likenesses that, if we tried to paraphrase them, would have no clear limit.

Davidson doesn't make any distinction between literary and non-literary uses of metaphor; 'Metaphor,' he says, 'is a legitimate device not only in literature but in science, philosophy, and the law' (31). This is quite true, of course, but it doesn't follow that the reader of a scientific treatise encountering a metaphor will treat it, or be treated by it, in the same way as the reader of a poem would. In the former, the reader will seek to close down the potentially endless implications to produce something clear and firm; in the latter, the reader will allow the metaphor to do its work relatively unhindered by such expectations. Nor does Davidson escape the 'deviation' model, basing it on the patent *falsity* of the sentence containing a metaphor: 'Generally it is only when a sentence is taken to be false that we accept it as a metaphor and start to hunt out the hidden implication. (...) Absurdity or contradiction in a metaphorical sentence guarantees we won't believe it and invites us, under proper circumstances, to take the sentence metaphorically' (40). This is a somewhat disappointing conclusion after the promising idea that the words in metaphorical sentences mean what they normally mean; the relation between sentences and the world they refer to has now become the key to the movement into a metaphoric register. But patently false statements are not hard to find in literary works (Davidson clearly doesn't mean the kind of false statement that is normal in *any* fictional language); we could turn not only to folk and fairy tales, romance and fantasy, but also to the genre of 'magic realism', whose effectiveness relies on our *not* taking the patently absurd goings-on as merely metaphorical.

A better sense of how metaphors impress themselves on the reader comes from a passing comment Davidson makes on novelty: 'What we call the element of novelty or surprise in a metaphor is a built-in aesthetic feature we can experience again and again, like the surprise in Haydn's Symphony no. 94 or a familiar deceptive cadence' (36). Leaving aside the problems Davidson introduces by using the word 'aesthetic', this statement points to the *sequentiality* which is a necessary part of the experience of metaphor. If, as I am arguing, metaphor in literary works, when read as literature, is *performed*, the opening up of semantic (and thence emotive and even somatic) possibilities is a product of the relation between one word and the next, one phrase or sentence and the next. There is, it seems to me, a continuum along which sequences of words invite greater or lesser inventiveness on the part of the reader because they conform more or less fully to the expectations encoded in the language. Davidson's model may work for Hume, where we register immediately that the philosopher cannot possibly be talking about kings and their enemies and so allow their metaphoric implications to come into play; but in literary works we are constantly alert to resonances that take us away, perhaps only a very short distance, perhaps very far indeed, from the most straightforward meanings and uses of language.[16] I want to hold on to Davidson's idea that the words in metaphors mean what they usually mean, and Sperber and Wilson's insistence that metaphors require no special interpretative procedures; but I want to add that our experience of literary metaphors involves an enjoyment of the powers of metaphoricity as it expands the possibilities of language.

★ ★ ★

A further claim I made in *The Singularity of Literature* was that responding to a work of art is an activity with an *ethical* dimension. This may seem strange, given that I've been stressing art's staging of the processes whereby we engage with the world, each other, and ourselves, as distinct from the direct engagement that occurs outside art, and that one might assume was the domain of the ethical. However, what I've said about art's capacity to introduce alterity into the settled framework of our lives should indicate that I'm not proposing to re-introduce the notion of art-for-art's sake or championing the autonomy of the art object. The point I would stress about the ethical — and the political — significance of art is that although it has profound effects in the world, these can never be predicted in advance, and that this is a constitutive impossibility. If the effect of the other could be known in advance, it would not be other. So art, in the strict sense, is pretty useless as a political tool — which is not to say that the objects we call artworks haven't been and won't continue to be immensely valuable in political struggles, just that this value depends on their capacity to be used in ways other than the artistic.

My focus, however, is on the reader. What does it mean to 'do justice' to a work of art, to use a common phrase that has clear ethical implications? Or, to return to the somewhat narrower topic of this essay, to do justice to a work of literature? In the first place, it means doing justice, as we've seen, to the work's singularity, inventiveness, and alterity, and this means finding some means to respond with an answering singularity, inventiveness, and alterity. Indeed, there is a sense in which it is only in such inventive responses that the work *comes into existence* — as an act/event — at all. In this response, I have already argued, we are responding to the invention of the artist or artists, in two senses: what has been created, and the process of creation itself. We are therefore responding to the work (again in both senses) of another person. (For simplicity's sake, I shall stay with the assumption of a single writer, though everything I'm saying could apply to a group or a series of writers). And the impulse to do justice to the work, which means to make it happen anew (and always differently) in one's reading of it, is an ethical impulse: in Levinasian terms, to respond to the other not as a generalizable set of features or a statistic but as a singularity. Levinas's term for the singular other, appearing before me and obliging me to take responsibility for it, is the *face* — and his use of the term is not metaphorical, although it is not simply literal either. We might extend the notion of the face, and the obligation it imposes, to the concrete, specific, ungeneralizable work of art.

Now let us pose the question with regard to the specific phenomenon of literary metaphor. I've chosen a well-known passage by Shakespeare, because I want to keep alive the dual question of inventiveness, alterity, and singularity over time and over several readings. The passage was written some four hundred years ago, and most readers will already have encountered it several times: under these twin conditions, can it still be said to introduce the other into the same, to surprise by its inventiveness and alterity? And if so, how does one do justice to it as a literary work? More specifically, how does one do justice to its metaphors? How do we perform metaphors, or the figurative potential of language, in a passage such as this? (Of course, in concentrating on the working of metaphors I'm leaving out a great deal more that could be said: for example, I'm not making any attempt to see the passage in its historical context, which would be an important part of a full reading.)

> *Enter* JULIET *above at her window*
> But soft, what light through yonder window breaks?
> It is the east, and Juliet is the sun.
> Arise, fair sun, and kill the envious moon,
> Who is already sick and pale with grief
> That thou, her maid, art far more fair than she.
> Be not her maid, since she is envious;
> Her vestal livery is but sick and green,

And none but fools do wear it; cast it off.
It is my lady, O, it is my love!
O that she knew she were!
She speaks, yet she says nothing; what of that?
Her eye discourses, I will answer it.
I am too bold, 'tis not to me she speaks.
Two of the fairest stars in all the heaven,
Having some business, do entreat her eyes
To twinkle in their spheres till they return.
What if her eyes were there, they in her head?
The brightness of her cheek would shame those stars,
As daylight doth a lamp; her eyes in heaven
Would through the airy region stream so bright
That birds would sing and think it were not night.

(Act II, scene ii, 2– 22)[17]

A literary work may be performed in many ways. It may be read silently or aloud, or experienced in someone else's performance — and in the case of a play-text, that can range from a straightforward reading to a full theatrical production or a film. If someone else is performing it, and we are responding to that performance in a way that brings to bear on it our own creativity, we can still said to be performing it ourselves, in the extended sense in which I am using the word in this essay. We are not simply interpreting it, discarding the husk of form for the kernel of meaning. For the purposes of this discussion, let us imagine that we are reading *Romeo and Juliet* aloud, and have reached the moment when Romeo looks up at Juliet's window not long before dawn.

When I, as a literary critic, comment in writing on a literary work I have read or heard I may offer an interpretation or a description, or I may go further and attempt to convey the work's singularity, inventiveness, and alterity in my particular time and place by taking my readers through the experience of performing, and being performed by, the work. Such a commentary will succeed only if it finds readers who, in their turn, will read it responsively and creatively, in conjunction with a similar reading of the original. And by responding creatively I don't mean freely associating; I mean affirming inventiveness by an answering inventiveness, whether enunciated or unarticulated, that is prompted by the specificity and special value of the work. In this sense, a full response to a literary work is a responsible one.

★ ★ ★

The first line of the speech appears to be unmetaphorical: Romeo observes a lighted window in the darkness. However, the word 'breaks' seem to me (I won't hide behind a generalized 'we' or 'the reader') charged with a degree of metaphorical suggestiveness: this light not only breaks through the window — the *OED* allows the meaning 'penetrates', continuing its definition, 'as light breaks the darkness' — but also conjures up the idea of *daybreak*. What also suggests some expansion beyond the literal is the grammatical form of the line: one would think that there is no mystery about a light in an upper room at night, yet this light seems to be, for this viewer, unusual enough to provoke a question. This slight enigma impels me onto the next line, where the answer to the question reveals that, although one could hardly call the unorthodox use of a question a metaphor, something like a metaphoric understanding of the light was already stirring in the previous line — what I took there to be the shining of a candle or a lamp (with perhaps overtones of the onset of dawn) is to be retrospectively understood as the radiance of a girl's beauty.

To comment in this manner is to imply that in reading line 1 I don't know what will come in line 2; this is of course not true after my first encounter with the speech, but it captures the fact that the lines *stage* enigmas and resolutions, metaphorical expansions, and so on: these events are still effective on the hundredth reading precisely because they are not simply using these linguistic capabilities but showing them off in a sequential process. (If I wanted to complicate the reading further, I could discuss the interplay between knowing what lies ahead and performing a certain ignorance of it.)

The metaphor, when it comes, is as plain as any metaphor could be, expressed in the simplest diction and syntax (contrasting with the inversion of the previous line): 'It is the east, and Juliet is the sun'. If the words mean what they usually mean, as Davidson encourages us to think, they invite me to imagine, and share, a frame of mind in which a window can also be a horizon, and a woman can also be the rising sun; the frame of mind of a man suddenly, desperately in love. And at the same time, because I'm not overhearing a scene taking place next door but reading a literary work, I take pleasure in the operation of the metaphor, in its surprisingness, its directness, its charge of satisfaction as it helps to make sense of the previous line. Another way of putting this is that I am aware of a source of this language that is not Romeo (though it is an awareness that I don't bring into full consciousness most of the time); there is an author, about whom it would be possible for me to know nothing except that this line is his invention, and that in responding to the line I am responding to the act/event whereby he invented it. My responsibility as a reader is to this author, not as flesh-and-blood man but as he is to be found in the line, as well as to the singularity and alterity of his invention.

A further dimension to the metaphor is the range of other metaphors it calls up, that panoply of literary figurations in which the beloved, human or divine, is the sun. It is no ordinary metaphor: Derrida devotes careful attention to the solar metaphor in 'White Mythology', calling it the 'paradigm of the sensory *and* of metaphor'.[18] Yet what is so surprising about this particular manifestation of the metaphor is its elementariness, as if all those elaborate comparisons were falsifications and unnecessary hyperbole: quite simply, 'Juliet is the sun'.

Although the line seems to close in on itself in its simplicity and directness, the following lines open up and develop the metaphor (and thus increase the force of its metaphoricity): 'Arise, fair sun, and kill the envious moon,/Who is already sick and pale with grief'. I find myself taken on a strange semantic journey, in which an image of a beautiful girl looking out of a window at the night sky fuses with an image of the rising sun diminishing the brightness of the moon. 'Arise' belongs the first of these images, but suggests 'rise', belonging to the second; 'fair' belongs to the first (we wouldn't normally call the sun 'fair'), but 'sun' to the second. 'Kill' then comes as a particular surprise, a metaphor *within* a metaphor, a human action being used of an astronomical body itself standing for a person, but in its murderous suggestion taking me into a new semantic domain rather than back to the girl standing at the window. That domain continues to govern 'envious', as human attributes now spread to the moon — presumably not only a metaphorical moon to match the metaphorical sun, but the real moon, that both Romeo (and perhaps Juliet) can see in the sky above. The oddness of 'envious' is then given some justification in a new conceit: the specific quality of the moon's light, 'sick and pale', is ascribed to its envy — its envy of the sun (within the metaphor of sunrise) and of Juliet's sun-like radiance (within the half-metaphoric, half-literal representation of the scene itself).

The emotional tonality of the speech is further complicated by the wish on Romeo's part that the real sun should *not* rise (not many lines later Juliet is saying ''Tis almost morning, I would have thee gone', and Romeo is observing how 'The grey-ey'd morn smiles on the frowning night'). If only Juliet were the sole sun, the joy of the moment would not be darkened by an awareness of the literal sun, about to rise. The unexpected violence of 'kill', and the imputation of envy to the moon, feed into this sense of hostile forces all around — for of course daylight implies discovery by the Capulets.

In the next line, the metaphorical sun turns back into something closer to the literal Juliet, now not a sun-like beauty but a virgin devoted to chastity: the moon's envy, it turns out, as the conceit is given a further unanticipated turn, is that of the mistress outdone by a follower — 'That thou her maid art far more fair than she'. Yet some lingering sense that the girl remains sun-like is provided by the repetition of the word 'fair', now yoked in memory with 'sun'. Romeo is beginning to play with his metaphorical scheme now, as is Shakespeare; and the reader who is enjoying the lines (rather than finding them an inaccurate representation of what a lovestruck youth might actually say to himself) is enjoying the sport as well.

But if Romeo's verbal games seem unrealistic, that aura of courtly rhetoric is shattered by the note of sexual urgency in the next line: although the metaphor is further extended, it is now used to express unambiguous desire for physical union: 'Be not her maid, since she is envious'. Of course, the second half of that line is completely spurious as argument, because the moon's envy is something Romeo has just invented; but desire does not necessarily appeal to logic to justify itself. It is as if the metaphor he has been developing as an expression of his delight has suddenly struck him as having some potential as a tool of seduction, though there's no denying the joke (and the joke itself is partly a joke about the power of metaphor). The metaphor is then further extended — 'her vestal livery is but sick and green' — with the moon now standing for the ideal of virginity, and virginity itself troped as an ill-coloured outfit (with hints of the maid's traditional green-sickness and the jester's motley). Romeo's urgent appeal that gives the extended conceit its climax — 'cast it off' — is a metaphor that threatens to become literal, as the young man looks at the girl dressed, no doubt, for bed.

My experience of that final injunction is of the metaphoric urge exhausting itself as the very literal fact of desire takes over, and the three lines that follow are all the more powerful in their resistance of metaphoricity, as critics have often noted and actors recognized. But soon the metaphors reappear, this time in a more fanciful guise as Romeo indulges in a little narrative; I am now made aware not so much of the power of language to express emotion through metaphor, but of the extraordinary capacity of metaphorical language to take leave of the observed world. I find myself enjoying the excessive elaboration of the 'eyes as stars' metaphor ('having some business' is a wonderfully down-to-earth note to strike in connection with astral imagery) just as much as the representation of ocular beauty that is to be relished. This is metaphor revelling in metaphoricity.

★ ★ ★

I've tried to give some sense of how I participate in this passage's inventive metaphors as I read it, performing, and enjoying, the metaphors as metaphors while responding to their evocation of human emotion. Although I've read it dozens of times, I find as I re-read it in order to write about it, it remains surprising, not quite the familiar passage I had remembered. I don't make any great claims for this reading, except to the extent that it is motivated by a desire to affirm the inventiveness and singularity of the passage, to bring it into the realm of the familiar — the discourse of literary criticism, for instance — while preserving its otherness. This is what I take to be the aim of a responsible, and hence ethical, reading; an attempt to do justice to the work, the work that has survived four centuries (by not remaining the same) and the work that someone called William Shakespeare undertook, or found himself undertaking.

DEREK ATTRIDGE

NOTES

1   Derek Attridge, *The Singularity of Literature* (London, Routledge, 2004).

2   Among the numerous works of Derrida's that have influenced my thinking about literature, I might single out 'Psyche: Invention of the Other', the interview ' "This Strange Institution Called Literature" ', both in *Acts of Literature*, edited by Derek Attridge (New York, Routledge, 1992), and *The Gift of Death*, translated by David Wills (Chicago, University of Chicago Press, 1995), especially chapters 3 and 4.

3   Maurice Blanchot, *The Space of Literature*, translated by Ann Smock (Lincoln, University of Nebraska Press, 1982), 202.

4   See ' "This Strange Institution" ', 44–50. Paul Ricoeur also uses this term in analyzing the operation of metaphor, though in the service of a more conventional account of the two levels of sense, the literal and the metaphorical; see *The Rule of Metaphor*, translated by Robert Czerny (Toronto, University of Toronto Press, 1977), 221.

5   This apparently straightforward statement conceals, of course, a complex set of much-debated issues. To elaborate a little: we call something fictional when there is no *necessary* relation between its assertions and assumptions and the world we inhabit. If the sun rises in the east in a fictional work, this is not because it has to.

6   Roman Jakobson, 'Closing Statement, from the Viewpoint of Linguistics: Linguistics and Poetics', in *Style in Language*, edited by Thomas A. Sebeok (Cambridge, Mass., M.I.T. Press, 1960), 350–77.

7   I am using the term 'metaphor' in a fairly general sense to refer to the creative use of language whereby a fresh semantic alignment — one that is not already coded in the language — is achieved, whether on the basis of similarity (metaphor in the strict sense), contiguity and association (metonymy), or part-whole relations (synecdoche). To place metaphor and metonymy in opposition, as Jakobson famously did (and Lacan equally famously after him), seems to me to obscure their similarity as tools for the enlargement of the semantic, and perhaps emotive, range of the language.

8   David Hume, *A Treatise of Human Nature* (London, J. M. Dent, 1911), volume I, 182.

9   Robert Graves, *Collected Poems 1965* (London, Cassell, 1965), 280.

10   See, for example, George Lakoff and Mark Johnson, *Metaphors We Live By* (Chicago, University of Chicago Press, 1980), Raymond W. Gibbs, Jr., *The Poetics of Mind: Figurative Thought, Language, and Understanding* (Cambridge, Cambridge University Press, 1994) and Mark Turner, *The Literary Mind* (New York, Oxford University Press, 1996).

11   Ronald Carter, *Language and Creativity: The Art of Common Talk* (London, Routledge, 2004).

12   This is the first line of Ted Hughes's poem 'Wind', *Collected Poems*, edited by Paul Keegan (London, Faber and Faber, 2003), 36.

13   Dan Sperber and Deirdre Wilson, *Relevance: Communication and Cognition* (Cambridge, Harvard University Press, 1988), 231–7. See also Diane Blakemore, *Understanding Utterances: An Introduction to Pragmatics* (Oxford, Blackwell, 1992), 160–4.

14   Thus the speaker, we are told, will 'adopt, on different occasions, a more or less faithful interpretation of her thoughts' (237): the literal is faithful, the metaphoric faithless.

15   First published in *Critical Inquiry* in 1978, reprinted in Sheldon Sacks, ed., *On Metaphor* (Chicago: University of Chicago Press, 1979), 29–45, from which I am quoting, and included in Davidson's *Inquiries into Truth and Interpretation* (Oxford: Oxford University Press, 1984).

16   I have made use of Davidson's essay in discussing J. M. Coetzee's use of allegory; see *J. M. Coetzee and the Ethics of Reading: Literature in the Event* (Chicago: University of Chicago Press, 2004), chapter 2.

17   William Shakespeare, *Romeo and Juliet*, *The Riverside Shakespeare*, ed. G. Blakemore Evans (Boston: Houghton Mifflin, 1974), 1068.

18   Jacques Derrida, 'White Mythology: Metaphor in the Text of Philosophy', *Margins of Philosophy*, translated by Alan Bass (Chicago: University of Chicago Press, 1982), 250.

Qu'est-ce que la littérature pense? (Literary Thinking)

It wouldn't be hard to say what literature knows. It knows the generic human subject. It knows its failings, its weaknesses and, on the basis of that knowledge, transforms the inevitability of resignation. Resignation to the fact that, as in one of the very first examples of the *Bildungsroman*, *Wilhelm Meister's Apprenticeship*, the world never lives up to the Idea; or, as in the earliest naturalist novels, by Zola, resignation in the face of ignominious social conditions. In its lowest form, this is knowledge of a sort of dismal moderation of the real, compared with the wild assertions of theory — and of philosophy, in particular. Literature knows inside out the workings of deceit, ungratefulness, selfishness and stupidity. Literature serves as a 'critique'; it is often praised for its aggressive or morose insights, or congratulated on its 'lucidity' when, like Céline, it aspires to make 'little music' of our wretchedness.

Even Proust, as fine a writer as he may be, spends a very long time, and a great many volumes, exploring the interminable web of degradation and vanity, cruelty and resentment, absurdity, smugness and murky, innermost sentiments, before finding salvation in the Second Coming of writing. Before discovering the only thing that matters — and which marks the transition from knowledge to thought: the victories of which humanity is capable. The 'supra-sensual hour' that James describes in connexion with the hero of *The Ambassadors*, Beckett's 'blessed times of blue', in *How It Is*, the enchanted death of Prince Andrew in *War and Peace*, Julie's testament in *The New Eloise*, the peasants' procession around the wounded airmen in Malraux's *Days of Hope*. . . or Conrad's novel, entitled simply *Victory*.

The idea that literature thinks, and that writers might be thinkers, as Natacha Michel argues in an essay on contemporary prose, can only mean that it opens up the realm of the particular: subtle psychological insights, social differences and cultural specificities, to the field of knowledge. For that must mean, as we know from experience when a novel secures a victory in our own minds, that literature's effect takes place at the level of thought.

What should the word 'thought' be taken to mean in this instance? First of all, that there is an encounter with a real, beyond the fictional world, which is its triumph, and at the peril of language, which is its Assumption.

Beyond the fictional world, literature that thinks emerges in the cracks in the story (*la fable*). It has no interest in wrecking the story, in contradicting it or pulling it to pieces. It accepts the story and settles down in the spaces it leaves.

I will turn briefly to my own work as a novelist. In *Calme bloc ici-bas* (1998), I borrowed the form and characters for the story (*fable*), as well as the relation between story and History (*le rapport de la petite histoire à la grande Histoire*), from Victor Hugo's novel, *Les Misérables*. But I pulled apart the building blocks of the narrative, rearranged the spaces, and allowed my prose to explore areas outside its initial scope. I employed language in three distinct registers — narrative, rhetoric and shorthand — in the hope that a few grains of real would emerge from this clash of styles.

In the essay to which I referred earlier, Natacha Michel proposes another method: that of allowing an 'other' language to take root in the language itself, with the reader witnessing the birth of a unique language.

In any case, the complicity of fiction and language aims to mark the real with the seal of the unique, of the One, of that which has never taken place prior to this complicity (this work) and will never appear again.

Literature thinks insomuch as it brands a real pursued by fiction with the symbolic scar of the One.

This gives rise to an essentially finite quality — common, in fact, to all artistic procedures — encapsulated in the word 'work' (of art) (*oeuvre*). There is the 'unique language' of the writer; the binding of every work in the form of a Book, even if, as Mallarmé preferred, it is in 'several volumes'; the double meaning of the word 'end': that signified by the word at the bottom of the last page, and that which the literary enterprise is compelled to bring to any sequence, whether we like it or not, and, last but not least, the standard of perfection. A work of literature is such — must, indivisibly, be such — that nothing in it can be changed. Each and every word of its prose is irreplaceable.

In stark contrast to the infinite variety of experience (which is perfectly obvious), the work of art or literature is the difficult, unlikely production of the finite. And it is precisely this production that constitutes thought.

The maxim of art-thought is simple: to produce something finite (artificial) to rival the infinite (natural).

I used the words 'work of art or literature', but what does 'literature' actually mean? Literature is a singular configuration which, unlike poetry, tends not to appear in the ranking of fine arts. In his analysis of categories of nineteenth-century aesthetics, Jacques Rancière makes some striking observations on the genealogy of modern meanings of the word 'literature'. Not only does it fail to obtain the patronage of any of the Muses of classicism, but it cuts across literary genres: clearly, 'literature' cannot be confined to poetry, but neither is it restricted to the novel, the story or the essay. It refers to the development of a sort of literary exception in the field of art. The concept of this exception gradually takes shape in France, from Baudelaire to Blanchot, with contributions from Flaubert and Proust, although Lacoue-Labarthe and Nancy, in a book entitled, significantly, *The Literary Absolute*, have shown that it originated in Germany or, more precisely, German romanticism. Writing is conferred absolute status by the exception, which not only raises it above classical genres, but puts it entirely beyond the scope of the empirical world. Thus, literature is an immanent reference to itself, a mark of its own self-sufficiency. It comprises Flaubert's prose, which, thanks to its style (a crucial operator in literature), the author intended to exist in its own right, with no imaginary referent in the world. It might equally be one of Mallarmé's sonnets, which he described as 'a fact, a being, happening by itself' (*fait, étant, il a lieu tout seul*), or conceiving perfectly of itself.

Of course, the advent of literature also corresponds to the emergence of a literary conscience, a conscience not exactly comparable to artistic judgement, since it relates not to rules of taste but to the conviction of the existence of an entirely separate phenomenon: literature (*le fait littéraire*), as compact and distinct as an Idea.

But doesn't this Ideal separation, obtained through stylistic density alone, require the Idea to be fully self-conscious? In other words, if literature is a form of thought, mustn't it be the thought of that thought? We know about Mallarmé's revelation, or the crucial experience that inspires his poetry: 'My thought has thought itself, and I am but a corpse'. This means that the poem as absolute requires it to be the thought of the thought that it is *and* that the author should be excluded, since the author merely imagines the basic Idea, leaving it to deploy the various facets of its self-reflection: 'since the Master went to draw tears from the Styx'.

But if literature's role is to allow fulfilment of the Idea as thought of thought, the author's task must not only be to marry his or her style with the initial production of the basic Idea, but also to ensure, explain, and stage the coming-into-being of the Idea as thought. Thus, literature is always accompanied by successive Manifestos of its becoming-absolute. The age of literature is also the age of literary manifestos, combining a diagnosis of the time (from Mallarmé's 'Crisis of Verse' to Natacha Michel's 'second modernity', not forgetting Breton's prophecy ('Beauty shall be convulsive or shall not be at all')) and a preferred procedure (hermeticism, self-reflexive writing, metaphor...) which, at any one time, contains the essence of the literary phenomenon.

We can therefore make the following assertion: that what literature thinks is both a real marked in language with the seal of the One, and the conditions governing the way that real is marked. The thought process of writing is the conjunction, under the finite sign of the One, of the autonomous forces of language and the immanent occurrence of a real.

There are two questions to be asked about literature:

With regard to the real: what takes place, which is not from the empirical world, which is 'anywhere outside the world', and which is worth organizing into thought so that it can be encountered beyond the fictional world?

With regard to language: what takes place in the language, which might be equivalent to the real that-which-has-taken-place?

Literature can be represented as a graph with two axes, neither of which is literary *per se*.

The first axis corresponds to the real as that-which-has-taken-place, or the non-empirical essence of all reality. Although it is left out of any ordinary story or prefabricated narrative, this is the real of which literature must speak. I do not believe, as Blanchot sometimes suggests, that this is the original silence with which all language draws strength from the infinite. The point is to open up to the realm of thought the singularity of whatever takes place outside that realm. Literature is a direct contradiction of Wittgenstein's axiom ('Whereof one cannot speak, thereof one must be silent'), since its first, essentially non-literary, axis is the imperative to speak of the unspeakable of that-which-has-taken-place.

The second axis is language, as a flexible resource with infinite power, by all means, but not, in this case, employed for what it is capable of saying, rather exploited mercilessly for what it has not yet said, or what it has always been reluctant or unable to say. Writers are the torturers of language; they extract confessions and even, perhaps — and therein comes the danger — lies.

The literary act—sometimes called 'writing'—is like plotting a graph along these two axes. It can be drawn as follows:

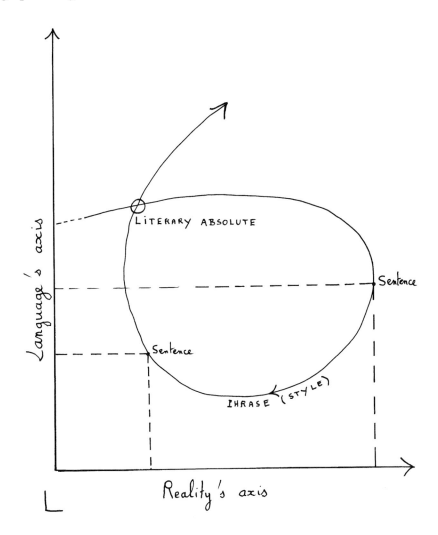

Every point along the graph can be called a 'sentence' (*phrase*). Each sentence indexes a real to a break in language. The active movement that joins two sentences together (with other sentences) can be called 'phrasing' (*phrasé*). The laws that govern phrasing, which only become discernible afterwards, can be called the 'style'.

The truly remarkable thing is that the graph of the literary act is always closed in places: a closed area (or areas) exist(s), because certain points are always drawn twice, becoming double points. If no such points exist, then the literary act constitutes a failure: the infinite dissemination of its linear emptiness; the total absence of the real; boring prose and conventional style.

The double point means three things.

It repeats language, at a particular point in its own expression. Let's say that it produces knowledge of its creative innocence and, in so doing, puts an end to that innocence. For the perverse aspect of the double point is that literary desire is always, at least at some point, knowledge of its own form; a kind of calculated self-interest inflicted upon innocence.

It asserts that thought is also thought of thought, turning its own thinking, at least in places, into a closed area, and a glimpse of the gap between inside and outside. The literary act commemorates its journey with a monument.

Lastly, it shows the same real point twice, making it impossible to discern from that point the beginning of the movement and the point that is ultimately reached. Like Proust's madeleine, the real point becomes an absolute, in which it is impossible to distinguish origin from destination. It escapes situation in time. It is, in the literary work itself, the scar of its eternity.

In fact, this point is what we encounter in a work of literature, far beyond what we read there. It is the literary act itself, transmitted, and submitted, to us (for in this case transmission and submission are one and the same). It fulfils the pre-Socratic maxim: 'It is all one to me where I begin; for I will come back again there'. This double point is the symbolic seal of the One, the real of the real, which is also, to use James's lovely expression, 'the figure in the carpet'. It was to him that the Romantics gave the most appropriate, and extravagant, of names: the literary absolute, which belongs to all eternal writing.

ALAIN BADIOU

(Translated by Alistair Clarke)

The Facticity of the Literary Work

Contemporary criticism and the poetic and critical tradition, in their various forms since Antiquity, may of course be read for what they are and according to the explicit definitions they offer of literature. They must also be read as arguments which define, by their own limits, a particular characterization of literature, which must be seen as implicit or implied since this characterization is legible from these very limits. This approach allows us to specify the minimum conditions for the identification of literature and its inevitable function: the questioning of symbolization and social representations; hence revealing the significance of literature without positing various states of literature, or idealizing it, or dismantling its identification or its identity.[1]

i. Concerning the Relinquishment of the Literary Work

Contemporary criticism and its characterizations of literature express a relinquishment (*délaissement*) of the literary work. This relinquishment can be found in various critical approaches, whether the emphasis is on the relation between the work and the author, the work and the reader, the work and its objects, or the autonomy of the work. In each of these instances the emphasis laid on the second term is inextricably linked to a certain relinquishment of the literary work, illustrated here simply by the relation between the work and the objects it acknowledges as its own. The opposite theories of mimesis and anti-mimesis start from the same question: what the literary work can be referred to. This implies that the literary work can be characterized either according to its determination — but then the question of the literary work's heteronomy with regard to the world remains unaddressed; or according to the kind of 'alternative world' it constitutes — but then that leaves unanswered the question of the relevance of the literary work. There is, in both cases, a relinquishment of the literary work. From this perspective, the emphasis laid on the autonomy of the work can be interpreted as a response to the ambiguities inherent in these various critical approaches and to the questions that they leave unanswered. The hypothesis of the relinquishment of the literary work is necessary, however, if one wishes to conceptualize the work's autonomy: it prescribes *what* the work is but precludes any interpretation of its 'raison d'être'. Criticism implies that the literary work can only be considered objectively to the extent that none of its thought processes (*actes de pensée*) within the aforementioned critical paradigms can express the 'raison d'être' of the literary work. It is clearly impossible to determine the 'raison d'être' of the literary work from the work itself; one can only acknowledge the reality of the work and this reality can seem uncertain. This explains why, within the perspective of the autonomy of the literary work, the work is identified as performative. It also explains why the notion of writing in a given literary work can be linked to a characterization both according to form and according to its performative nature. Contemporary criticism is still attached, whether implicitly or explicitly, to the main tendencies of the poetic and critical tradition. In this tradition, the identification of the literary work relies on heterogeneous arguments: it is identified with a form, or with beauty, or with the idea of beauty, or with the work's means; in other words, the various poetic and technical characterizations of the work. These modes of identification raise the same questions about the relation between the literary work and the author, the object, or the reader, and the same questions about its identity, as contemporary criticism. It is the self-evidence of the form of the literary work that makes it difficult to describe the passage from the author to the work. It is the acknowledgment of the beautiful that justifies the endless string of interpretations. It is the attention paid to literary devices, integral to any thinking about form and beauty, that enables us to see the work as autonomous. It is the consistency of implicit or explicit reference to form, beauty, and such devices, that raises the question of the relation between the literary work and its object.

ii. *Presentation, Quantity*

These various critical approaches define a paradoxical availability of literature. This is traditionally expressed through the distinction between a work — which is marked by a certain unavailability — and a product — which lends itself to use and makes itself available. It is also expressed in terms of the uncertainty of meaning, which is taken to be the main characteristic of the literary work, or in terms of the surplus of meaning which is to be expected from the literary work. Meaning is therefore what is not decisively available but may, however, be so. This ambivalence, shared by the various contemporary critical stances, is eventually expressed in terms of the recognition of the supplementary nature of writing. The contemporary prevalence of the signifier confirms this: the foregrounding of the signifier is the method of the literary work, which reveals the paradox of availability and meaning. The various critical angles are ways of restoring an operative and symbolic dimension to that work, through the acknowledgment of its unavailability — in other words, ways of postulating a form of availability, following the recognition of unavailability.

This recognition of the paradoxical availability of the literary work must be reinterpreted as the recognition of its facticity: the literary work is available only through its unavailability; it inevitably lays itself open; it is a self-constituting fact and therefore by the same token its own presentation.[2] The various critical approaches constitute oblique responses to the recognition of this presentation. The fact that contemporary criticism seldom refers to beauty, that it even assumes its negation, does not alter the fact that it implies the recognition of a presentation tied to a specific perception. Thus, contemporary nominalism is no more than the ultimate expression of a nominalist tradition which tells us that language is the language of literature, and that it enforces its law on literature.[3] This tradition intimates against its own principles: since the literary work exploits the limits and constraints of its material (language and its laws), the literary work is a presentation of this and of itself. This is actually the hypothesis of most contemporary formalisms, even when they deny these implications or any nominalist bias. It is therefore necessary to insist on the fact that the literary work is presentation and facticity. That contemporary criticism cannot be dissociated from the relinquishment of the literary work implies the self-evidence of the literary work; it implicitly recognizes the facticity of the work; it can express it only through the inconsistencies in its own arguments.

The poetic and critical tradition also implies presentation. Thus, the identification of literature with a form means that we must identify and describe in the literary work the movement from linguistic material to form. Here lies in essence the recognition of the constitution of the presentation of the literary work, reduced to formal conditions which are in turn indissociable from a process, this movement from matter to form. Matter is given a form, which can be either linguistic or semantic. Therefore the characterization of the literary work in relation to language can be understood in these terms: the literary work is this very material — language — and the process appropriate to this material; and this accounts for presentation. Therefore the identification of literature with beauty, the idea of the beautiful, or the realism of beauty, implies that the literary work is presentation and that the autonomy of this presentation stems from a specific perception, which can be subsumed under the universality of beauty. Thus all the technical characterizations of the literary work, in terms of particular rules, devices, genres, or imitations, imply once more an autonomous presentation, stemming from a specific perception, which can be subsumed under the consistency of processes, and the generalization that imitation implies. Identifications of the literary work, as proposed by the critical and poetic tradition, are inseparably linked with the fact of presentation, although they do not examine it in detail. This link is confirmed by arguments about the effects of the literary work, which are in turn inseparable from these identifications of literature or the literary work.

This conclusion, drawn from contemporary criticism and the poetic and critical tradition, about the sense in which the work constitutes a presentation, prompts two remarks. *First*: presentation is, for the author and for the reader, the minimal characteristic which guarantees the identification of the literary work. *Secondly*: this same characteristic enables us to offer a minimal definition of the relation between the author and the work, and the work and the reader. These two relations can be characterized in the same way: the literary work is presentation to a consciousness. It is unnecessary to qualify the relation of the reader to presentation in any other way than in terms of consciousness — presentation is destined to be perceived as such, and therefore implies a perceiving consciousness. It is also unnecessary to characterize the relation of the author to presentation in any other terms than the following: the author conceives of the literary work as presentation to a consciousness. Thus to define the relation of the reader and the author to presentation amounts to emphasizing the necessity of the link between author, work and reader, without becoming embroiled in any of the ambiguities of contemporary criticism and the poetic and critical tradition. Unearthing these similarities between contemporary criticism and the poetic and critical tradition, and their inbuilt suppositions, enables us once more to remark: the work presents itself as self-evident and it asserts the validity of this presentation against all other discourses and its own conditions. The literary work precludes any competition from other discourses and imposes itself on the reader.

The arguments of contemporary criticism and the poetic and critical tradition are ones that the literary work acknowledges as its own or that are acknowledged as such. They are merely contributions to the signal that the literary work gives, or that must be attributed to the work, and whose existence those arguments therefore presuppose: the literary work is presentation but also quantity. The notion of quantity implies that presentation cannot be dissociated from a kind of absolute magnitude that the work possesses, thanks to which it imposes itself on one's consciousness. In other words, the literary work may be thought of as the signal that it is that very thing. Thus to infer, from contemporary criticism and the poetic and critical tradition, the quantity of the literary work, enables us to make two further observations: *the first concerns attention* which, in accordance with its quantity, is supplementary to the perception of the literary work as presentation to a consciousness. *The second concerns the relation of the literary work to its object*: in accordance with its quantity, the work surpasses any object it acknowledges or that is acknowledged as its own. This has been expressed in many ways throughout literary history. To identify the literary work with the arbitrariness of the sign or with the signifier is just the most recent way of recognizing the fact of the quantity of the literary work.

The various approaches to the literary work found in contemporary criticism, with different relations to its object, or to the reader, all presuppose an indissoluble link between presentation and quantity, which create the authority of the literary work, and establish that these relations exist in accordance with the fact of the literary work, its presentation, its quantity. The poetic and critical tradition, in its various versions, characterizes the literary work as a kind of supplement to its linguistic and semantic material, and as the realization of something that has its own intrinsic value and has no equivalent — beauty; and as the presentation for its own sake of its own material. The literary work, characterized in this way, holds its own against any other discourse, because it is in itself a realization which implies a condition, but overcomes this condition.

At this stage, two conclusions can be drawn. *First conclusion*: being its own fact, presentation, and quantity, the literary work can display a variety of forms, genres, or even a lack of explicit literary marks. Following this line of thought, the characterization of the literature of the signifier must be interpreted as the epitome of the identification of presentation and quantity. *Second conclusion*: being its own fact, presentation and quantity, the literary work disrupts any discourse that attempts to establish its ability or inability to represent ideas, or truth, or its fictitious or non-fictitious character.

The various discourses on the literary work's truth or lack of truth, on its ability or inability to represent the Idea, on its fictitious or non-fictitious character, imply that one can distinguish a presentation that symbolizes a given idea from one that perverts it, a presentation that can state its truth from one that cannot, a presentation that prescribes its own relation to reality from one that does not. These various discourses correspond not to variations in the literary work's properties or status, but to various evaluations according to various contextualizations, whether implicit or explicit, based on their recognition of the self-evidence and quantity of the work. Following the general trend of the poetic and critical tradition, the sort of play that effects this disruption can of course be interpreted as the play of *mimesis*. However, any recognition of the play of *mimesis*, like any attempt to take account of the reactions of the reader or the spectator, relies on the identification of presentation and quantity, and the recognition that this presentation is presentation to a consciousness — in other words to a subject who can participate reflexively in the recognition of this presentation and quantity.

Presentation and quantity are expressed through the self-evident devices of literary works. *Through the interplay of closure and threshold:* the theatrical stage, whether the stage of classical theatre, the Shake-spearean stage, or the Italian stage, presents a closed structure, which conceals what remains exterior to it. In much the same way, the thresholds of the literary work — beginning and end — represent the impossibility of evaluating the literary work according to its context, or the representation of such a context. Through the *form and the singularity* of the literary work: on the one hand the emphasis laid on form implies that the material which is thus 'informed' is still present in that form; on the other, the emphasis laid on technique means that the literary work is treated as the illustration of its own material. In both cases, the material is displayed by the literary work at the same time as that work asserts its independence from other examples and from any blunt apprehension of the material, an independence achieved through the work's specific realization. *Mutatis mutandis*, the same must be said of the characterization of the literary work in terms of its singularity: this singularity is a singularity of material, which, thus, is not presented for its own sake. These forms of recognition are implied without being made explicit by contemporary criticism and the poetic and critical tradition. *Contemporary criticism* expresses these recognitions through its double characterization of literary narrative (this is only an example): in terms of narratorial play involving several

types of narrator, which means associating the narrative with a particular communicative property; or in terms of the absence or near
absence of a narrator, in which case the narrative is characterized as
self-presenting or telling its own story, in some sense. *Poetic and critical
tradition* notes that the work can be a mere ornament.

The fact that these notions are only implied means that these
diverse characterizations and interpretations of literature and of literary
works impose upon them definitions which are entirely dependent on
whatever are held to be their determining conditions. In contemporary
criticism, these are the determinations of the object, the author,
the reader, and language — the autonomy of the literary work can
only be understood in relation to these determining factors. In the
poetic tradition, these are the determinations of the material, or of
reality, irrespective of the work's perceived relation to beauty. The
prominence granted to determination leads to propositions which are
contradictory in themselves. Thus, in contemporary criticism, to say
that literature is language, in other words that it is determined by
language, amounts on the one hand to identifying it with language
and its constraints, and on the other, characterizing it in terms of
the signifier, in other words defining it as a contingent linguistic fact.
Thus, in the poetic and critical tradition, beauty is often associated with
a form of naturalism — classical poetics — and with determination by
the real, inseparable from the sense of surprise, wherein the recognition
of contingency appears once again — Aristotle's *Poetics* recalls the fable
of Mitys.[4] These contradictions mean the literary work is marked by
indeterminacy. In contemporary criticism this is what is emphasized
by assertions concerning the lack of meaning, free meaning, or the
signifier, and in classical poetics, the recognition of the 'je ne sais quoi'.

iii. Information and Enunciation

To proceed along the implicit lines of contemporary criticism and
the poetic and critical tradition amounts to approaching the literary
work according to the paradoxes of its presentation and its quantity.
The presentation that the literary work constitutes is characterized
by its contrastive play with the status of discourse as defined in
standard communication — the latter implying an explicit context
and addressee. Standard communication has three aspects: information, enunciation and comprehension. These three aspects are
not dissociable and must be apprehended in their unity. The unity
of information and enunciation distinguishes communication from

simple information — for example, the information a perception gives to a subject. Hence, communication is the finalized presentation of information, effected by subjects. The unity of information, enunciation and comprehension defines the aim of communication: to seek the agreement of the addressee(s) about this information. This agreement becomes the means for another act of communication. By definition this agreement is not definitive — comprehension implies both an understanding of what is communicated and the possibility of agreeing or disagreeing on what is communicated. Besides the fact that communication, by virtue of the ever-present possibility of a new act of communication, represents its own continuity, the differences between speakers and the possibilities of agreeing or disagreeing also help make communication continuous. Communication, therefore, however it is realized and whatever its modes, always calls into question its object and the difference between speakers.

Conversely, the literary work may well be discourse and enunciation; it may well carry information and imply comprehension. It can, however, only be an explicit presentation if it undoes what prevents discourse from being presentation: the unity of information, enunciation and comprehension. The literary work creates a discrepancy between information and enunciation and marks them with a paradoxical difference. As a consequence, comprehension of the literary work cannot be represented and is not possible in terms of the comprehension that standard communication implies. The comprehension embodied by the literary work and the comprehension of this work are impossible without the acknowledgement of the duality of enunciation and information.

Lyric poetry is exemplary in this respect. Whether in the classical, medieval or romantic tradition, this sort of poetry consists in the act of addressing explicitly an identified or indeterminate other — the public. This is particularly the case with romantic lyric: private speech, by dint of a certain formal play, is presented as public speech; it presents itself as pertaining to the public sphere, even though it situates its *raison d'être* and its themes in the private sphere. Herein lies what is literally an impossibility — namely the singularity of a discourse which presents itself, however, as common speech; private speech presenting itself as public speech. Lyric poetry of this sort may see itself in terms of a form of communicational play — as in some of Hugo's addresses — but it cannot be equated with the play of standard communication, for two reasons. *First:* in standard communication, the information is, as a matter of principle, independent from the state of mind of the interlocutors—something lyric poetry fails to confirm. *Secondly*: in standard communication, enunciation cannot be dissociated from information. In lyric poetry, enunciation—the expressivity of a subject—is explicitly opposed to the 'universalizing' paradigms of this poetry, paradigms implied by information and its public sphere.

In much the same way, any literary narrative is an account of events, of past actions, of a past, in some instances explicitly dated; every literary narrative represents a narrative exchange without pragmatic commitment, and as such can always be actualized—it thus represents a present, the present of narration. The literary narrative, which involves no pragmatic commitment, can be seen as the presentation of a narrative exchange, which has to do with the difference between past and present and whose temporal markers remain undetermined despite the reference to the past. If a literary narrative constituted a strict actualization it wouldn't represent temporal difference—all narratives are narratives of the past. If it didn't present this past, through the narrative exchange, as a past that might be actualized, then it would not be presentation. Literary narrative is a narrative paradox: the narrative exchange implies the erasing of the pragmatic and contextual markers of this exchange. It is also a temporal paradox: as an actualized presentation of the past, it consequently does not present the past as past, although it remains, like all narratives, a narrative of the past. In other words, the means of communication do not aim at communication *per se*, but rather aim to prompt recognition of the presentation which the narrative constitutes. The presentation, in the present, of the past, which the narrative embodies, contradicts the very fact of information—that the past has passed. In this way there is a discrepancy between enunciation and information.

Similarly, theatrical representation makes use of paradoxical means. The temporality of the stage is at one with the temporality of the audience, in the same way as the theatrical space is one; the actors address the audience members, who are watching them. This unity is literally an impossibility, which emerges firstly in the division between the stage and the audience, secondly in the fact that the actor's gaze is not directed towards the audience—the audience is not seen by the stage but is involved in the projection of a gaze which seems to look beyond the audience and behind its back as it were, and thirdly, in one of the obvious consequences of this impossibility—the temporality of the performance is as it were exterior to the audience. This performance, the theatrical representation, is acknowledged as such by the audience and is the occasion of the transference of the presentation on the stage to a subject, the audience member, who applies his or her mind to that presentation and treats it as its own representation. This relation between the actor and the audience illustrates the dissociation of information and enunciation. It relies on the fact that the actor does not reveal in his own name the information carried by the text of the play. This too illustrates the dissociation between enunciation and information.

Finally, the paradox of this dissociation can be seen in what amounts to the minimum practice of discursive presentation: the resumption or repetition of a given discourse. This offers information, the information contained in that discourse; and there is an implied enunciation, which allows the possibility of resumption and reiteration. There is no obvious unity of enunciation and information — it is apparent from the possibility of repetition that the information is not specific to a particular enunciation.

This dissociation of information and enunciation is why the literary work as such doesn't finalize its own information or its own enunciation. Under these conditions, the comprehension which accompanies such a process (*un tel jeu*) cannot be defined according to the comprehension generally associated with standard communication.

Its initial condition is the acknowledgment of the dissociation of information from enunciation. This means that comprehension of the literary work cannot be finalized within the framework of the pursuit of communication. This dissociation of information from enunciation, as seen in relinquishment, form, beauty or devices, establishes the literary work as alterity and therefore identifies everything else as alterity in relation to the work. The dissociation of information and enunciation is fully functional only if the literary work is seen as distinctly underdetermined with regard to any possible context. This explains why this dissociation is inseparable from the play of quantity: this dissociation means one cannot comprehend the literary work's information in terms of a context to which such comprehension would be strictly bound. This explains why the literary work always calls for interpretation. It also rules out the possibility of finalizing our comprehension on the basis of explicit meanings and a limited number of contextual references occurring in the work; the meaning which can be attributed to a literary work remains highly abstract in relation to the letter of the work.

iv. Immediation, Mediation, Adherence

Because the literary work is presentation, presentation to a consciousness, and the play of quantity, it reveals itself according to an 'immediation' which is inseparable from a specific mediation. This mediation maintains an act of reading that does not contradict the fact of presentation.

Immediation: because the literary work is its own fact, presentation and quantity, it abides by a principle of duality and a principle of integrality. *Principle of duality*: the presentation that constitutes the literary work is self-presentation. It marks itself off from any form of representation conceptualized implicitly in the discourses of context, standard communication, and pragmatic exchange; and from any form of representation which the speakers involved in this context can respond to and debate in terms of validation or invalidation. As presentation, and therefore as distinct from any form of representation implied by standard communication, the literary work appears neither as a discourse determined by a context — irrespective of any context the work itself may bring into play — nor as a discourse determining a context. The *principle of integrality* means that the literary work is unique; it must, therefore, be taken to be complete, in the sense that, as presentation, and quantity, it is not expressed according to a pragmatic context. If it were to be expressed according to a pragmatic context, the uniqueness attributed to it would be characterized according to that context, according to the finality of the literary work in that context. To express the unity of the work one must first express this uniqueness.

These two principles shed light on the fact that the literary work can integrate, as presentation and quantity, current discourses, including those of other literary works, and therefore the appearance of the world as represented by those discourses. These principles tell us that the literary work has no particular relations imposed upon it and imposes none itself. The literary work cannot ultimately be identified in terms of its relation to the author or to the reader, or in terms of its level of literality, or explicitness, nor according to its representations. In other words, according to these two principles, the literary work can represent standard means of communication — what is expressed according to the implicit or explicit addressee of the literary work, according to the implied or represented narrator, the designated or implied reader. The work also presents itself as something that cannot be 'resolved' in the play of standard communication (even though it exposes that play) and as something that allows for the interplay of the reader's consciousness — a consciousness preoccupied with words, but also with what it perceives and with itself.

Immediation thus implies *mediation*. Outside any pragmatic context, the literary work ensures the possibility, for the reader or spectator, of recognizing the presentation it constitutes, and does so through the paradoxes, discussed earlier, which define its genre. This takes the form of the observation, external to the work, carried out by the reader, which is congruent with the internal observation that the work makes of itself; it also takes the form of the paradoxes attached to presentation and the thematization by the literary work of its quantity.

These two observations are expressed through the generic paradoxes associated with the discrepancy between information and enunciation. In *narrative* we find, on the one hand, observation, internal to the narrative, of the difference between the timeless actuality of the narrative and the narrated past — it is thus a matter of *poiesis* which appears for example in temporal metalepsis; and on the other hand, the observation of this *poiesis* occurs from a point external to the narrative — as a matter of reading. The recognition and the external observation of this actualization in the present are implied in the reception of any narrative which is not testimonial or historical. This external observation, carried out by the reader, is essential if the presentation that the narrative constitutes is to be identified in its specificity. In the *theatre*, we find observation, internal to the play itself, of the interplay of representation and its object, traditionally expressed through dramatic events and recognition. The spectator, who sees and knows fully all that the characters see and know only partially, sees and knows through external observation, which is exactly congruent with the process of internal observation. This external observation is essential to the restitution of the difference between the temporality of the theatrical representation and that of the audience, and in order that this theatrical representation be perceived as presentation to a consciousness, and that this recognition of the presentation be a recognition of the presentation as such. In *lyric poetry* the internal observation concerns enunciative shifts and the identification of the subjective enunciation with an *ethos* which, by definition, involves public or collective figures. External observation, in the case of a work of poetry, takes the form of the reader's questioning of the work's relation to the enunciator and to anyone else. This amounts to identifying lyric poetry as poetry wherein any reader can recognize, according to the presentation it constitutes, his own expression — this reveals again that poetry is presentation to a consciousness.

The interplay of double observation, prompted by presentation and requiring the dissociation of information and enunciation, has as its counterpart, where quantity is concerned, an act of *attention*, implied, presented and thematized by the literary work insofar as its signs work on two levels. Quantity becomes apparent through a certain duality: it is 'one', yet it exists only through the thematization of its construction, the heterogeneity and overlap of two sets of signs, namely the distinguishing or identifying markers of objects or agents, and the internalized signs, the signs of these objects or agents, which a given subject, as presented in the literary work, internalizes. Reading follows this heterogeneity and this overlap; the reader's attention is therefore captive but nonetheless free by virtue of the ambiguities of this interplay.

The *sublime* is the ultimate illustration of this interplay of two levels of signs. It is thematized through the association of distinguishing or identifying signs with the subject who, within the literary work, expresses or recognizes the sublime. This thematization links the indication, in the work, of what exceeds the quantity of this work, with the elevation of the mind, awe and fear. In other words, the representation of whatever exceeds the quantity the literary work recognizes as its own is represented by way of the interpreted or internalized sign. The distinguishing signs and the interpreted or interiorized signs overlap because they belong to the discourse of this subject who expresses or recognizes the sublime. Through this overlap, this subject represents, internally to the work, the way the quantity of the literary work must be read on two levels according to the measure of this quantity, and to what exceeds it. The sublime therefore obliges the reader's attention to run along dual lines — it commands attention to the quantity of the literary work, which implies the measure or the exceeding of this quantity. This is not to say that the relation of the reader to the literary work undoes the decontextualization of the presentation, since the reading is entirely defined by a relation of involvement of the reader in the work, according to the work, its quantity, and the exposition (best exemplified in the sublime) of this quantity, while the exteriority of the reader to the literary work is confirmed by the recognition of the measure and the exceeding of the quantity which the work of the sublime implies. Apart from the sublime, the great literary genres represent, in their different ways, the interaction of quantity and attention according to the duality of the distinguishing or identifying signs and the internalized signs. The literary work is, by virtue of this duality, the figuration of its own quantity, according to the constitutive paradox of its genre. This enables it to focus the attention of the reader or spectator.

The recognition of presentation and quantity thus mimics presentation and quantity themselves. Through its presentation and quantity, through the communicative interaction of immediation and mediation, and through the process of double observation, the literary work triggers the recognition of a double set of signs, and so acquires a specific rhetorical status. The reader's consciousness of the work is shaped by presentation and by a key implication of quantity and the dissociation of information and enunciation: namely that the literary work is only what the consciousness considers at that time. Consequently, presentation and quantity, whatever their form, define the literary work on the one hand as that which enables any reading mind to be adequate to it, according to the reflexive interaction set in motion by double observation, and according to a reading based on the interplay of distinguishing signs and internalized signs; and on the other hand, as the site of any possible recognition of its objects according to its presentation — which means that this recognition cannot be explicitly contextualized. Alien to persuasion, even though it may have an argumentative dimension, the literary work thus establishes a certain sort of rhetorical relation to the reader: a relation of *adherence*. If a reader is not persuaded of the validity of the implications of a given work, in terms of its pragmatic context, that does not mean that the reader doesn't adhere to the work: not being persuaded does not entail the rejection of the literary work which remains presentation to a consciousness so long as it is read according to the processes of double observation and the double set of signs. By the same token, if a reader assents to the implications of the literary work, it does not imply that the work has been treated as a primary form of persuasion: the adherence of a reader to the presentation of the literary work does not necessarily coincide with the assent given to that presentation.

v. The Unavoidable Function of the Literary Work and of Literature

To describe presentation, quantity and adherence in this way amounts to recognizing the rhetorical paradox of the literary work: the way it goes beyond its own tautology, and so governs a specific poetics and specific rhetorical interplay. To put it briefly, the work's means of exceeding tautology imply that it does not correspond to (*soit l'inconséquence de*) its own identification. The literary work is its own determination and indetermination; it contains areas of indeterminacy between what it is and what it is not; it is its own identity and the figuration of any other identity. It displays its presentation as involving two indeterminate horizons: its own and that of its environments. The fact that the literary work can exist alongside the indeterminacy of literary genres, and may bear no specifically literary marks yet still be deemed 'literary', underlines the constancy of the literary work. As both tautology, and that which goes beyond this tautology, figuring its zones of indeterminacy, the literary work redistributes the space of social representations and symbolizations. This redistribution of the space of social representations and symbolizations is indissociable from a questioning of the relation between given representations and symbolizations and a universal fact — as implied by the interplay of mediation and immediation. The fact that this redistribution is indissociable from a specific rhetoric means that social representations and symbolizations are self-questioning. The way that the literary work exists in accordance with the indetermination of literary genres and of literature, the way it radicalizes the lack of signifying intention — in the literature of the signifier — simply carries on the redistribution of social representations and symbolizations, and the same questioning process. The autonomous literary work is heterogeneous.

JEAN BESSIÈRE

(Translated by Yves Gilonne)

NOTES

1 This text offers a comment on contemporary debates which to a large extent are bound to be fruitless, since they remain determined by characterizations of literature which, because they do not address their own conditions, stand in the way of a clear view of the permanent function of literature. The remarks found here will be developed in my forthcoming publication: *Les Principes de la théorie littéraire* (Paris, PUF).

2 For a characterization of presentation in an argumentative perspective, see Chaïm Perelman, *La Nouvelle Rhétorique. Traité de l'argumentation* (Paris, PUF, 1958), volume I. Within this conceptual framework, and although Perelman does not offer such a definition, literary discourse is characterized as presentation without argumentation.

3 Although no specific nominalist approach to the literary work is available, the linguistic characterization of literature, which Barthes started promoting fifty-five years ago, and which many critics have reformulated many times, should be equated with a nominalist approach. For example, Genette's assertion that literature imitates language (*Figures* III) is a nominalist assertion.

4 Editor's note: the statue of Mitys at Argos fell on and killed the man who himself was responsible for Mitys' death. Aristotle alludes to this fable when discussing what makes a good plot in a tragedy, and writes 'even coincidences are most striking when they have an air of design (…) Plots, therefore, constructed on these principles are necessarily the best'. *Poetics* chapter 9 (available at http://classics.mit.edu/Aristotle/poetics.1.1.html).

Musical Thinking: Hegel and the Phenomenology of Prosody

Does 'musical thinking' exist? Is there a thinking, that is to say, which is not thinking about music, or thinking which accompanies music, but a thinking which takes place in music; a thinking which is made up of music itself? Perhaps even to put the question in this way seems strange. Yet if we can imagine that in written texts a thinking may take place which is not precisely the same as what their authors may have thought, in the sense that in every writing 'we meant something other than we meant to mean'; and if we remember that there is nothing in the letters, words, and sentences of our languages, considered as material, which of itself must inevitably signify anything at all; then it may be possible to wonder why, in so many circles, the idea that musical works have meanings, or that they are cognitive acts, the idea that music is a form of thinking, has come to be understood as a piece of 'metaphysics' or of 'ideology'.[1] My interest in this question develops partly out of my work on philosophers who have themselves been interested in it, partly out of my own amateur acquaintance with music, and partly out of my professional interest in the question of prosody: in how to reawaken an enquiry into the philosophical foundations of the study of that aspect of language, an enquiry which has long slumbered; in how to put prosody back at the centre of the way in which we think about poems and poetry; in how to understand prosody's elusive yet undeniable cognitive character. I want to take as my occasion for these reflections an examination of some aspects of the relation between language, music and thinking in Hegel's thought, because the idea of the relation between these terms which is given there provides an unusually careful examination and elaboration of a series of presuppositions which have for us to some extent become a kind of unexamined common sense. The apparently marginal topic of versification takes us, it will be suggested, to some central problems in Hegel's way of conceiving subjectivity. Hegel was capable, after all, of using the emergence of 'rhythm' from 'metre' and 'accent' as a figure for the speculative proposition itself (*PhG*, 38); this paper seeks, in particular, to develop with reference to a Hegelian example Henri Meschonnic's insight that 'There can be no theory of rhythm without a theory of the subject, and no theory of the subject without a theory of rhythm.'[2]

If, then, we admit the question of whether there is a thinking which is made up of music itself as a possible question, much in any answer will depend on the sense which is given to the word 'thinking'. One way of understanding that word, a way which at first appears to rule out the idea that there could be a thinking which is made up of music, is to take thinking as defined by the kind of 'making-explicit' which depends upon referentiality. From this point of view one might be likely to employ *music* as a figure for just that moment in any shape of spirit at which thinking had ceased or failed, and so to arrive at a pejorative sense for the idea of 'musical thinking'. Just such a moment is described by Hegel in part of his account of a so-called 'unhappy consciousness' in the *Phenomenology of Spirit*:

> In this first mode, therefore, where we consider it as pure consciousness, it does not *relate* itself as a *thinking* consciousness to its object, but, though it is indeed *in itself*, or implicitly, a pure thinking individuality, and its object is just this pure thinking (although the *relation of one to the other is not itself pure thinking*), it is only a movement *towards* thinking, and so is devotion. Its thinking as such is no more than the chaotic jingling of bells, or a mist of warm incense, a musical thinking that does not get as far as the Notion, which would be the sole, immanent objective mode of thought. This infinite, pure inner feeling does indeed come into possession of its object; but this does not make its appearance in conceptual form, not as something comprehended, and therefore appears as something alien. What we have here, then, is the inward movement of the pure heart which *feels* itself, but itself as agonizingly self-divided, the movement of an infinite yearning which is certain that its essence is such a pure heart, a pure *thinking* which *thinks* of itself as a *particular individuality*, certain of being known and recognized by this object, precisely because the latter thinks of itself as an individuality. At the same time, however, this essence is the unattainable *beyond* which, in being laid hold of, flees, or rather has already flown. (...) Where that 'other' is sought, it cannot be found, for it is supposed to be just a *beyond*, something that can *not* be found. (*PhG*, 131)

That last note, indeed, may to our ears only confirm the possibility that 'musical thinking' may really be a kind of thinking properly so called, because the attempt to think an other which is none the less imagined as radically heterogeneous to thought has been the explicitly avowed project of many of the most significant thinkers of our time; although, for Hegel, that would only confirm the extent to which the powerful reach of the kind of devotional consciousness analysed here stretches far into putatively secular life. The idea of 'musical thinking' here is prefaced by some props from the repertory of fantasized Papism: 'the chaotic jingling of bells, or a mist of warm incense'. In the background of this passage we may perhaps hear the echo of a suspicion which had often been voiced in the century preceding Hegel, the suspicion that music in church might be a kind of superstition or even of idolatry. The passage joins several others in Hegel's work in which what appears to be fearful is the possibility that the material which accompanies thinking might take over; that a language which is in any case all too likely to resemble a chaotic jingling of bells should actually become mere ringing or glossolalia. Why does this musical thinking 'not get as far as the Notion'? Because its making-explicit is blocked. It comes into possession of its object only as stolen goods, as it were, since the object does not make its appearance in conceptual form, not as something comprehended. This is musical thinking rather than thinking proper, for Hegel, therefore, to the precise extent that there is a twinned failure of making-explicit: from one point of view, and most obviously, the object is not properly thought *about* but only felt in thought; from another and no less important point of view, this musical thinking fails to make explicit *for itself* the way in which its own devotional agonies are grounded in a situation which it has itself brought about, so that unhappy consciousness takes the division which it has inflicted upon itself as though it were a sheer fact about the world. Musical thinking, then, is not so much not thinking at all as a preliminary movement towards thinking, a thinking which has left so much implicit as to leave in question whether it deserve the title of thinking.

If 'musical thinking' here, then, is thinking which differs from thinking proper by lacking referential explicitness, a critical role is clearly played in differentiating musical thinking from thinking proper by the idea of language.

Language is self-consciousness existing *for others*, self-consciousness which *as such* is immediately *present*, and as *this* self-consciousness is universal. It is the self that separates itself from itself, which as pure 'I = I' becomes objective to itself, which in this objectivity equally perceives itself as this self, just as it coalesces directly with other selves and becomes *their* self-consciousness. It perceives itself just as it is perceived by others, and the perceiving is just *existence* which has become a self. (*PhG*, 395)

Musical thinking nurses its own singularity, as it were, and does not learn the lesson which language performs for thinking-proper, the lesson that, just as everyone calls themselves 'I', so this supposed singularity is ubiquitous. Language, in this view, does not merely name a subject which is already there: to be a subject is to enter, as a later follower of Hegel put it, into the symbolic order. Language is the necessary form which explicitness takes, and it is the more emphatically so for Hegel in view of his rejection of the empiricist account of language. 'We *think* in names', as he trenchantly puts the matter in the *Encylopaedia Philosophy of Spirit*.[3] We do not first inductively assemble a series of impressions for which we then cast around for a word; rather, language is, in so far as we may be said to be thinking at all, always already available to us.

If language does all this for thinking, though, what do languages, in the plural, do? For languages' plurality confronts us with one of those potentially unsettling moments in Hegel's writing at which a universality (here, the universality of self-consciousness) is temporarily yoked by the copula to some forlorn particular. The comically bathetic objection that in fact everyone does not call him or herself I, but rather *ego, ich, je, io*, to restrict oneself only to a few European languages in which there happens to be some single word, rather than an inflection or a tone, corresponding to the English word 'I', misses the point as thoroughly as it could do, yet must also raise a problem for a thinking which points out as tirelessly as Hegel's does that 'contingency' is just a name for the point at which enquiry gives up. It is the problem which J.G. Hamann's *Metacritique of the Purism of Reason* had already raised, with the same impertinence, with respect to Kant's account of 'reason'.[4] A letter of Hamann's develops this metacriticism:

Tradition and language are the true elements of reason. Sounds and letters are the necessary condition of all relations, in which concepts can be intuited and compared. All signs of language and writing have therefore in terms of their matter only empirical reality; in terms of their form and meaning however a transcendental ideality, and their universality as well as their necessity depend upon tradition, as their accidental delimitation is arbitrary.[5]

Whether or not one shares Hamann's theological approach, the questions raised by his metacritique are hard to forget once they have been pointed out. Thinking about language remains 'musical', in Hegel's, pejorative, sense, to the extent that it fails to be thinking about *languages*: to the extent that it surrenders the body of language, the mere chaotic jingling of these letters and sounds, to a sphere of sheer 'arbitrariness', and thereby converts a legitimate 'we do not know' into a resigned and consoling 'we cannot know'.

With this it becomes clear that it is more difficult than might appear to separate thinking proper from musical thinking, and that it is so partly because language is always threatening to become music or worse. An especially sensitive area in this respect (and one which remains sensitive today) is versification. Hegel's treatment of it begins by vigorously contesting the idea that verse is a fetter. It is untrue, he remarks, that 'versification is a mere hindrance to the free outpouring of inspiration. A genuine artistic talent moves always in its sensuous element as in its very own, where it is at home; it neither hinders nor oppresses, but on the contrary it uplifts and carries.'[6] The words appear to allude to Kant's reminder in the introduction to the *Critique of Pure Reason* that what we think of as external restrictions upon reason may instead be the conditions of the possibility of experience: 'The light dove, in free flight cutting through the air the resistance of which it feels, could get the idea that it could do even better in airless space.'[7] Yet, Kant points out, the air's resistance is what supports the bird in flight. Resistance may be all that holds us up. This implies a rather different way of thinking about language's materiality. The body of language, which must be to say the bodies of languages, we must now conclude, is not that set of otherwise chaotic and meaningless contingencies which must simply be made to serve poetry, but rather poetry's elements or mediums, something like poetry's conditions of possibility. The problem clearly occurs to Hegel, since he argues that despite the way in which authentic artists move in a sensuous medium which bears them up, it nevertheless is the case that *this* sensuous medium is more arbitrary than most (*HA* II, 1012). What is more, a further problem supervenes, because the initial characterization of the poet who is borne up and sustained rather than merely imprisoned by the limitations of verse comes to look rather different in the light of the changing historical conditions which Hegel himself sets out. Here Hegel's discussion is remarkable, like so much of his work, for his inability to allow any particular problem to be treated as something too minute for philosophy to enquire into.

In this case the refusal of mere contingency is most strikingly manifested when Hegel comes to deal with the problem of the origin of rhyme, or rather, of the origin of rhyme's dominance in medieval and modern European versification. In a way wholly characteristic of Hegel various 'external' explanations — Arabic influence, the collapse of the Roman empire through barbarian invasion — are offered and then set aside in favour of an explanation which will carry the right sense of necessity: 'The more inward and spiritual the artistic imagination becomes, the more does it withdraw from this natural aspect which it cannot any longer idealize in a plastic way; and it is so concentrated in itself that it strips away the, as it were, corporeal side of the language and in what remains emphasizes only that wherein the spiritual *meaning* lies for the purpose of communication, and leaves the rest alone as insignificant by-play' (*HA* II, 1023). The advent of rhyme, it turns out, is part of a structural historical mutation which shares the shape analysed in the 'unhappy consciousness' section of the *Phenomenology*. The opening up of an unprecedented kind of interiority, an interiority which takes the world set over against it for the inessential, means that the side of nature, the bodily aspect of language, is now experienced not as the natural habitat for the ideas of poetry, but rather as something either unimportant or at least important only in so far as it emphasizes the intellectual content of poetry. Indeed Hegel thinks that what is often thought of as the shift from classical quantitative to accentual metre can be understood as part of this process of interiorization, as a result of which 'the chief meaning acquires so much weight that it draws the impress of the accent entirely on to itself alone; and since the emphasis and the chief meaning are linked together, this coincidence of the two does not make conspicuous but drowns the natural length or shortness of the other syllables.' (*HA* II, 1021) This has the effect of completely changing the relation between the intellectual and the material in verse. 'If now, as is the case in full measure with our modern mother-tongue for example, these roots lay claim to the accent almost exclusively for themselves, this is throughout a preponderating accent on the meaning or sense; but it is not a feature which involves freedom of the material, i.e. sound, or could afford a relationship between long, short and accented syllables independently of the idea contained in the words.' (*HA* II, 1021) What Hegel is elaborating is something like a dialectic of our mastery over linguistic material. The weight which interiority gives to intended meaning performs an instrumental recruitment of sound, so that accents now serve, in Hegel's view, to emphasize meaning, rather than allowing, in his very striking expression, the material to remain free — rather, that is, than allowing accent and quantity to be patterned in a way which is in direct service to no particular meaning but instead as what we might think of as a kind of 'free' beauty. What makes this a dialectic is that, as with many of Hegel's powerful contrasts between what he called 'classical' and 'romantic' art, meaning by these terms something quite different from whatever may be meant by them now (meaning, that is, something which is closer to the complex structural distinction between 'heteronomous' and 'autonomous' art made in

Marxist aesthetics than it is to any classification of styles or tendencies), the transition is neither lamented nor celebrated but understood as a mutation in which losses and gains are intimately co-dependent. From one point of view 'a rhythmic figuration of time-movement and accentuation, divorced from the root-syllable and its meaning, can no longer exist; and there is left, in distinction from the above-mentioned listening to the richness of sound and the duration of longs and shorts in their varied combinations, only a general hearing entirely captivated by the emphasized chief syllable which carries the weight of the meaning.' 'This compels us, as if fettered, not to go beyond the sense of each word' (*HA* II, 1021). From this angle the collapse of quantitative metre is a radical deafening of the prosodic ear. The hearkening to free material, possible when that material was thought of as thinking's natural dwelling, goes deaf when it is imagined as the sensuous and habitually sinful body of language (for Hegel closely associates the rise of rhyme with the rise of Christianity).

The emphasis on interior intentionality thus results in a peculiar fixation or imprisonment. Yet at the same time, this process could not be less like the rise of a sheer indifference to the body of language. It is rather an obsessive investment of it with a new kind of power. In a strange way the diminished plasticity of post-classical versification in fact results in a newly intensified focus on sound in verse: 'because *romantic* poetry as such strikes more strongly the soul-laden note of feeling, it is engrossed more deeply in playing with the now independent sounds and notes of letters, syllables and words, and it proceeds to please itself in their sounds which, now with deep feeling, now with the architectonic and intellectual ingenuity of music, it can distinguish, relate to one another, and interlace with one another' (*HA* II, 1023). Hegel seizes, as so often in his thinking about Christianity, something of that pattern analysed by Peter Brown, in which the deep suspicion of the body in early Christian thinking by no means results in regarding the body as something indifferent, but rather transforms the body into a privileged place in which the signs and traces of the divine or the demonic are gloriously or terrifyingly manifested.[8] In this connection we may see that Hegel is very far indeed from regarding the advent of rhyme merely as a relatively unimportant result of the tearing-open of interiority. Since its origins are *necessary*, rather than external, we may view rhyme, even, as one aspect of the conditions of possibility of that interiority — and this because, as becomes clear, it can in a certain sense be said that the *subject* rhymes, for Hegel. Since it is of course not at all the case for Hegel that there are no subjects before Christianity or Roman law, but only the case that the particular conception of individual interiority which accompanies those social formations needs them to develop in the way that it does, it is already the case that the shape of versification in general, whether quantitative or accentual, answers to a need of the structure of human subjectivity as such: 'The I requires self-concentration, a return to self out of the steady flux of time, and this it apprehends only through specific time–units, struck just as markedly as they succeed one another and end according to a rule' (*HA* II, 1016, translation modified). The subject is a self-exteriorization and a return, a recollection after an excursion, for which language furnishes the most eminent model, but which is also seen, for example, in the structure of human labour. Only this excursion and return can convert the merely indifferent flow of time into the shaped and understood duration which makes subjectivity intelligible.

These requirements become both more acute and more problematic when the rupture of interiority associated with Christianity and Roman law takes hold. Rhyme is part of what allows a subjectivity thus conceived to sustain itself: 'The need of the soul to apprehend itself is emphasized more fully, and it is satisfied by the assonance of rhyme which is indifferent to the firmly regulated time-measure and has the sole function of bringing us back to ourselves through the return of the same sounds. In this way the versification approaches what is as such musical, i.e. the sound of interiority, and it is freed from the materiality, so to say, of language, i.e. that natural measurement of longs and shorts' (*HA* II, 1023, translation modified). If all versification satisfies the subject's need to collect itself out of any mere flow of dimensionless points of time, rhyme does this in a way peculiarly adapted to this historically individual shape of interiority: the *Gleichklingeln* of rhyme rings us back to ourselves in a way which is indifferent to firmly regulated measurements of time. Rhyme marks off the time of innerness against the world's time. Rhyme, through the return of similar sounds, does not merely lead us back to those sounds. It leads us back to ourselves. Rhyme is part of what makes Christian and ultimately modern subjects possible. The musical thinking of the 'unhappy consciousness' here chimes with the approximation of verse to the musical as such. And at this point we are given a striking definition of what the musical *as such* might be: the sound of interiority.

Yet what *is* the interiority which is to sound? The analysis of the 'unhappy consciousness' may already have warned us that interiority can be thought of as being 'nothing at all' without its objectifications. Since music is incapable of the kind of referentiality or representation offered not only by language but also by painting and sculpture, it becomes a question whether its proper field is anything at all either:

> Stone and colouring receive the forms of a broad and variegated world of objects and portray them as they actually exist; sounds cannot do this. On this account what alone is fitted for expression in music is the object-free inner life, abstract subjectivity as such. This is our entirely empty self, the self without any further content. Consequently the chief task of music consists in making resound, not the objective world itself, but, on the contrary, the manner in which the inmost self is moved to the depths of its personality and conscious soul. (*HA* II, 891)

It is hard not to be aware of a clash of emphases in this passage. On the one hand what music expresses is something 'entirely empty', something which has no content. On the other hand this entire emptiness is 'the inmost self', 'moved to the depths of its personality and conscious soul'. Since it is hard to imagine in what sense a purely *abstract* subjectivity, or an entirely *empty* one, may possess such innernesses, depths, and chasms, it is hard to escape the implication that there is something constitutively illusory about what it is that music attempts to express. Insofar as it must express abstract subjectivity, there is nothing at all to express. Yet the illusion of pure interiority is a real illusion, a shape of feeling which is really present, and for this reason it is not the case that it has no cognitive content, but that, like 'musical thinking' in the *Phenomenology*, it is a movement towards which does not 'reach as far' as cognition. Because Hegel's phenomenology is one in which any cut and dried opposition between feeling and knowing comes undone, the apparent non-existence of what music is to express comes undone too.

This is evident in Hegel's account of the connection between music and time. Time offers the ideal occasion for the negative nature of subjectivity to be explicated:

> The inner life in virtue of its subjective unity is the active negation of accidental juxtaposition in space...The similarly ideal negative activity in its sphere of externality is *time*. For (i) it extinguishes the accidental juxtaposition of things in space and draws their continuity together into a point of time, into a 'now'. But (ii) the point of time proves at once to be its own negation, since, as soon as *this* 'now' is, it supersedes itself by passing into another 'now' and therefore reveals its negative activity. (iii) On account of externality, the element in which time moves, no truly *subjective* unity is established between the first point of time

and the second by which it has been superseded; on the contrary, the 'now' still remains always the *same* in its alteration; for each point of time is a 'now' just as little distinguished from the other, regarded as merely a point of time, as the abstract self is from the object in which it cancels itself and, since this object is only the empty self itself, in which it closes with itself. (*HA* II, 907)

The impossibility of imagining real duration coincides with the impossibility of imagining a reality proper to the subject. Both, for Hegel, can only be conceived as acts of negation, as negativity itself. Yet what follows? This emptiness upon emptiness is shaped in just the right way for music to take a powerful grip. Nothing moves nothing, inexorably. 'Now since time, and not space as such, provides the essential element in which sound gains existence in respect of its musical value, and since the time of the sound is that of the subject too, sound on this principle penetrates the self, grips it in its simplest being, and by means of the temporal movement and its rhythm sets the self in motion'. It is with a sense of disbelief that we read the single-sentence paragraph which concludes this section. 'This is what can be advanced as the essential reason for the elemental might of music' (*HA* II, 908). It is apparent that it strikes Hegel too as insufficient, because he immediately goes on to qualify the 'essentiality' of this 'reason': 'If music is to exercise its full effect, more is required than purely abstract sound in a temporal movement. The second thing to be added is a *content*, i.e. a spiritual feeling felt by the heart, and the soul of this content expressed in notes' (*HA* II, 908).

The extent to which the apparent nothingness of abstract subjectivity, a nothingness which music is to express, always and necessarily spills over into a rich, moving and complex 'something' in Hegel's account of music is reinforced by the extent to which, as the analysis of 'musical thinking' in the 'unhappy consciousness' section has already suggested, Hegel thinks of musical and religious feeling themselves as being deeply kindred shapes of spirit:

What constitutes the real depth of the note-series is the fact that it goes on even to essential oppositions and does not fight shy of their sharpness and discordance. For the true Concept is an inherent unity, though not a merely immediate one but one essentially split internally and falling apart into contradictions. On these lines, for example, in my *Logic* I have expounded the Concept as subjectivity, but this subjectivity, as an ideal transparent unity, is lifted into its opposite, i.e. objectivity; indeed, as what is purely ideal, it is itself only one-sided and particular, retaining contrasted with itself something different and opposed to it, namely objectivity; and it is only genuine subjectivity if it enters this opposition and then overcomes and dissolves it. In the actual world too there are higher natures who are given power to endure the grief of inner opposition and to conquer it. If music is to express artistically both the inner meaning and the subjective feeling of the deepest things, e.g. of religion and in particular the Christian religion in which the abysses of grief form a principal part, it must possess in the sphere of its notes the means capable of representing the battle of opposites. These means it gains in the so-called dissonant chords of the seventh and ninth, but what these indicate more specifically is a matter on which I cannot enter further here. (*HA* II, 927–8)

This presents a substantial elaboration, and perhaps a modification, of the view which Hegel has initially advanced, that the entirely empty self is what music expresses, because it works from an opposition between abstract and 'genuine' subjectivity. The modification becomes clearest at the point at which Hegel suggests that, in dissonance, music actually possesses the means of *representing* a battle of opposites. What music is representing in such dissonance is implicitly regarded as more than a merely subjective set of feelings; it is implicitly compared to the capacity of, for example, the *Science of Logic* to make the necessity of undergoing contradiction, rather than the abolition or evasion or deletion of contradiction, the principle of its own organization. There are subjects who can live through contradiction without going under; and, it is further suggested, there is music which can give expression to this ability to undergo contradiction. The passage resonates contrastively with the pejorative account of 'musical thinking' in the analysis of the 'unhappy consciousness', because it appears to suggest that music can in a certain sense represent and thus *know*, rather than symptomatizing, the contradictory character of unhappy consciousness.

This, then, is where this particular conception of thinking and, with it, this particular conception of subjectivity, has brought us on the question of 'musical thinking'. Music has served as a figure both for the failure of thinking to become fully explicit, and for an interiority which misrecognizes its imprisoned or sheltered innerness as a natural fate. It has been able to serve in this fashion because what is meant by thinking here is this excursion and return; because the subject, in other words, must objectify itself even in order to be a subject. It is nothing at all without recognition: no cognition without re-cognition! In so far as music begins to take on an implicit cognitive content, it can do so only to the extent that it too follows this pattern. There could be musical thinking which is thinking proper only in so far as music can in some way become representation.

If music cannot become reflection, recognition, and representation, there can be no musical thinking. One of the reasons for following this train of interconnections through at such length has been that, far from being an untypical or exotic way of thinking about the subject, this aspect of Hegel's work chimes with the default mode of modern anti-metaphysical metaphysics. That is to say, wherever thinking and subjectivity are still appealed to all, it is usually with a series of precautionary defences against the least hint of a supposedly 'metaphysical' soul talk. What must above all be made clear when we talk about the subject is that we are not designating anything which has any being: we are rather talking of a form, an activity, a negativity, or a linguistic position or trope. Otherwise we are worshipping that worst of idols: the thing which thinks.

Let us now consider, however, whether this is what thinking must mean, and whether this is the way in which subjectivity must be conceived.

It is true that no one can be certain that he is thinking or that he exists unless he knows what thought is and what existence is. But this does not require reflective knowledge, or the kind of knowledge that is acquired by means of demonstrations; still less does it require knowledge of reflective knowledge, i.e. knowing that we know, and knowing that we know that we know, and so on *ad infinitum*. This kind of knowledge cannot possibly be obtained about anything. It is quite sufficient that we should know it by that internal awareness which always precedes reflective knowledge.[9]

Here, then, thinking does not at all mean the same as making-explicit.

9. *What is meant by thought.* By the term 'thought', I understand everything which we are aware of as happening within us, in so far as we have awareness of it. Hence, *thinking* is to be identified here not merely with understanding, willing and imagining, but also with sensory awareness. For if I say 'I am seeing, or I am walking, therefore I exist', and take this as applying to vision or walking as bodily activities, then the conclusion is not absolutely certain. This is because, as often happens during sleep, it is possible for me to think I am seeing or walking, though my eyes are closed and I am not moving about; such thoughts might even be possible if I had no body at all. But if I take 'seeing' or 'walking' to apply to the actual sense or awareness of seeing or walking, then the conclusion is quite certain, since it relates to the mind, which alone has the sensation or thought that it is seeing or walking.[10]

As the phenomenological strand of French Cartesian scholarship has been energetically pointing out over the last couple of decades, passages such as these do not fit comfortably with the usual maps of what Descartes did to us all.[11] Yes, the opposition between mind and body is every bit as sharp as is generally lamented. But what counts as 'mind', what counts as thinking is, as soon as one begins to enquire closely into it, strikingly bodily. Heidegger's belief, for example, a belief so influential for all our subsequent anti-Cartesianisms, the belief that the cogito is a model of reflection, of representation, of recognition, is in fact a fundamentally mistaken one. What grounds my being is not reflection, knowing that I know, thinking that I think, and it is thus not at all anything emptied of affectivity; it is rather the primordial fact of affectivity itself in so far as I am affect. The feeling of thinking, as the feeling which *I — am*, and not thinking about thinking. Insofar as I am my body, rather than having it, this body is part of thinking.

Without judging at all, for the moment, whether such an idea of thinking is legitimate, one thing which we can notice is the impossibility, within such an idea, of identifying thinking with making-explicit, or with that aspect of language which is identified with such making-explicit. The block upon offering any content at all to subjectivity, on pain of a relapse into soul-talk, has in fact left us with a much more idealist notion of the subject and of thinking as our default model. And it is perhaps this kind of idealism — a sober, non-metaphysical, indeed an anti-metaphysical, almost, it may be thought, a *materialist* kind of idealism — which forms the most serious obstacle, currently, to recognizing the thinking that goes on in prosody. What this essay must end by invoking, therefore, could in no way be a series of solutions to questions about the nature of prosodic cognition, but rather some suggestions about how the questions themselves might be realigned. First of all, there need not be any reason why the possibility that prosodic aspects of poems be bearers of meanings in their own right should depend upon the possibility of establishing a close analogy with *linguistic* meaning. If we can imagine forms of thinking and knowing which are not linguistic, and which do not rest upon linguistic modes of making-explicit, then we are also in that act imagining meanings and ways of meaning which are not like the relation of a signifier to a signified. So fully has a certain pan-linguisticism become the element within which cultural enquiry takes place, and within which it shelters from militant scientistic naturalisms, that the very notion of meaning without signifiers and signifieds may seem alien to us. But its ground is simple. In the meaning borne by the experiences of pain, fear, desire or hunger — those experiences which I cannot pretend I am not having, however hard my scepticism tries to help me — is grounded the possibility of any meaning whatever. Secondly, this then frees enquiry to explore the significance of prosodic aspects of language from a different perspective. Such exploration will surely have much to learn from a phenomenological approach, provided that phenomenology can be conducted in such a way as to register, rather than wrongly to bracket out, everything in my musical or prosodic experience which constitutes its real concrete complexity; everything, that is to say, which criticism, calling it personal, idiosyncratic, or unrepresentative, usually takes pains to strike out first off as a preliminary step towards the securing of objectivity. Only if we start from those musical and prosodic experiences which we actually have, rather than from their publicly respectable stuffed replicas, may we hope to find a less pejorative sense, not only for 'musical', but also for poetic, thinking.

SIMON JARVIS

NOTES

1 'We learn by experience that we meant something other than we meant to mean'. G.W.F. Hegel, *Phenomenology of Spirit* (henceforth *PhG*), translated by A.V. Miller (Oxford, Oxford University Press, 1977), 39.
2 Henri Meschonnic, *Critique du rythme: anthropologie historique du langage* (Lagrasse, Editions Verdier, 1982), 71.
3 Hegel, *Philosophy of Mind*, translated by William Wallace and A.V. Miller (Oxford, Clarendon Press, 1971), 220.
4 Translation in Gwen Griffith Dickson, *Hamann's Relational Metacriticism* (Berlin and New York, Walter De Gruyter, 1995), 523–4.
5 Dickson, 272.
6 *Hegel's Aesthetics*, translated by T.M. Knox (henceforth *HA*) (2 volumes, Oxford, Clarendon Press, 1975), II, 1012–13.
7 Immanuel Kant, *Critique of Pure Reason*, edited and translated by Paul Guyer and Allen Wood (Cambridge, Cambridge University Press, 1998), 129 (B140).
8 Peter Brown, *The Body and Society: Men, Women, and Sexual Renunciation in Early Christianity* (New York, Columbia University Press, 1988).
9 René Descartes, 'Author's replies to the sixth set of objections', in *The Philosophical Writings of Descartes*, translated by John Cottingham, Robert Stoothoff, Dugald Murdoch (3 volumes, Cambridge, Cambridge University Press, 1984), II, 285.

10 Descartes, 'Principles of Philosophy. Part One', in *Philosophical Writings*, 1: 195.

11 Cf. in particular, Michel Henry, *Genealogy of Psychoanalysis*, translated by Douglas Brick (Stanford, Stanford University Press, 1993); Jean–Luc Marion, *Cartesian Questions. Method and Metaphysics* (Chicago, University of Chicago Press, 1999).

Reflections on the Excess of Empire in Tayeb Salih's *Season of Migration to the North*

Both before and for some time after decolonization colonial literatures were in large received by metropolitan audiences as a source of
information about the unfamiliar locations, lives and psyches of distant
peoples. Subsequently and despite their variety, such writings were
subject to categorical interpretations as contesting European representation, initiating the genre of marvellous realism, advancing the
claims of identity, or registering a post-independence disappointment.
More recently critics attentive to both the historical substance and the
aesthetics of fiction have been concerned to devise a methodology
able to accommodate the formal sophistication of novels where the
referential saturates the fiction but cannot be grasped outside its stylistic
mediations. Tayeb Salih's *Season of Migration to the North*, published
in Beirut in 1967 and in an English translation in 1969, is one such
elaborately orchestrated work that self-consciously inscribes reflections on the medium and uncertainties of narrative.[1] Simultaneously
a melancholic evocation of a rural community in sub-Saharan Africa,
a melodramatic tale of Arabian days and nights in the equator and the
English North, and a critique of colonialism, its singular unfolding of
theme and meaning makes it at once legible and opaque.

Because I am not a student of Arabic literatures and the novel
is only available to me in translation, I am aware that the reading
I am about to propose requires some justification.[2] My pretext is
that the inseparability of the political and the literary in *Season* is of
moment to studying postcolonial fiction with appropriate regard for
the interpenetration of cognitive and aesthetic dimensions. By offering
a view on the metropolitan world from the colonial hinterland, and
on a colonial hinterland in the throes of social turmoil, cultural
upheaval and existential crisis, *Season* dramatizes the trauma of a
peripheral modernity, and does so in an innovative form that calls on
traditional Arabic and contemporary European narrative conventions,
joining poetry and prose, disposing of antique modes of story-telling
in order to deliver timely meditations on present dilemmas, and hence
containing a polyphony of discrete and competing voices.

When accounting for the 'power and possibilities' of high modernism, Fredric Jameson has located its conditions of possibility in 'the coexistence of realities from radically different moments in history' — a concept derived from Ernest Bloch's observation of 'the simultaneity of the nonsimultaneous', the 'synchronicity of the non-synchronous', although used by the two thinkers to very different ends and with distinctive implications.[3] Such incommensurability structures a novel where existence is marked by the discontinuous temporalities attendant on the precipitate and selective introduction of capitalist modes of production into pre- or nascent capitalist societies. *Season* is thus inhabited by a consciousness not only of the unevenness between the metropolitan and the peripheral, but by the disjunctions within the colonial environment where the socialities, cultural forms, cognitive traditions, affective inclinations and ethical sensibilities of both the ancestral and the modern overlap.[4] In this sense the book can be seen as staging a scenario which theorists have abstractly proposed as the conjunctural, but in no way seamless, relationship between material modernization, the ideological and psychological processes of modernity and modernism, this last, it has been suggested, providing a vocabulary for the lived experience of radical social and psychic transformation.[5]

Since the novel juxtaposes the mundane and the enigmatic, the recognizable and the improbable, the seasonal and the eccentric, the earthborn and the fabulous, its disparate discourses invite and frustrate a realist reading, demanding instead a reception able to hold these contradictory registers within one inclusive response. If we follow the thinking of Herbert Marcuse, a Marxist whose theories of the literary insisted on revaluing the realms of subjective consciousness and the unconscious, then the dialectic between the novel's perception of the historical world and the transfiguration of the empirical realm into fiction can be seen as emerging from the power of aesthetic form to estrange and subvert the quotidian by 'accusing' dominant social practices and ordinary modes of consciousness. For Marcuse moreover,

the radical qualities of art, that is to say, its indictment of the established reality and its invocation of the beautiful image (*schöner Schein*) of liberation are grounded precisely in the dimensions where art *transcends* its social determination and emancipates itself from the given universe of discourse and behavior while preserving its overwhelming presence.[6]

In the spirit of this model I will suggest that whereas Salih's narrative cannot be properly read without attending to its specific cultural materials or its historical representations and resonances, these can only be retrieved from their reincarnations as narrative and trope. So too Marcuse's assertion that literature can constitute 'a subterranean rebellion against the social order' by revealing 'tabooed and repressed dimensions of reality' (19, 20) enables an insight into the novel's unprecedented, startling and problematic critique of modern empire, a critique that inheres in an analogy between colonialist insult and violence and a degrading and death-driven eroticism. This matter of the book's 'counter-consciousness' in conjuring up 'modes of perception, imagination, gestures' that shatter 'everyday experience' (Marcuse, 19) is one to which I will return.

The two distinctive but interrelated stories of Mustafa Sa'eed and the narrator during their migrations to the north are told in the hieratic oral style of a *hakawati*, a public teller of tales in the Arab world.[7] The traditional beginning, 'You will recall, gentlemen...' is echoed by the narrator in the novel's first line ('It was, gentlemen, after a long absence (...) that I returned to my people'), and repeated in the course of his recitation to auditors apparently unfamiliar with both the obscure village on the Nile and cosmopolitan London. This conceit permits a storyteller licensed to combine fact and fable and speak in riddles, to include in his delivery description, transcription, digression and reflections on life and death. Moreover the deployment of this popular mode coexists, as Barbara Harlow has suggested, with mimicry of the Arabic literary technique of *mu-arada* (or *mu^cdradah*), a form literally meaning opposition or contradiction in which at least two voices participate, the first composing a poem that the second will undo by writing along the same lines, but reversing the meaning.[8] In this way, *Season* tells two interrelated but contrasting stories, one about deracination and intemperance and the other about rootedness and restraint. Mustafa Sa'eed's journey from the Sudan to London is a stylized tale of natal displacement, alienation from the English and revenge against the North, pieced together and reworked by the narrator from the spoken and written words of a tormented immoralist and an angry anti-colonialist consumed by *ressentiment* — a concept, according to Fredric Jameson, devised by late-nineteenth century ideology to explain not only the revolt of mobs, but also the revolutionary vocation of disaffected intellectuals.[9]

As recounted by the narrator, this biography, which is an interested interpretation of another's recounted experiences, is intertwined and contrasted with sober recollection of his own disciplined term as a graduate student in England and his responsible return to Sudan where he immerses himself in the educational system of the newly independent regime. 'I am from here', he tells his listeners, 'I too had lived with them. But I had lived with them superficially, neither loving nor hating them' (49). The interplay of discordant sentiments performed by the two voices extends to the internal tensions of a narrator torn between allegiance to home and envy of the wider vistas available to his counterpart, troubled by an illicit love, and disturbed by a growing disenchantment with village norms. Yet although he comes to fear Mustafa Sa'eed not only as his adversary but his double, and whereas his own story is as confessional and conflicted as the tale he mediates, his stance is programmed by the novel's borrowed form to remain in opposition to that of his double and antagonist. He thus seeks to distance himself from the other's quest for meanings of a 'deeper significance' beyond those offered by Sudan (66), castigating this as the 'pursuit of a foreign mirage' (93), and after reading Mustapha Sa'eed's fragmentary disclosures, withdraws from his minatory influence: 'I left him talking (...) I did not let him complete the story' (166).

Acknowledging the debate between 'traditionalism' and 'Westernism' in postcolonial Arab discourse, Saree Makdisi has argued that the novel 'shatters the very terms of this opposition' as it comes to occupy a zone between cultures.[10] This is a designation I find inadequate to the book's representation of the archaic within modernity and inappropriate to the unresolved duel of voices about the security and constraints of filiation and the liberating unease of dislocation. On returning from his studies in England, the narrator is delighted by the genius of his birth-place: he observes that 'the sound of the wind passing through palm-trees is different from when it passes through fields of corn' (2), concedes 'I must be one of those birds that exist only in one region of the world' (49), is gratified at the organic composition of his grandfather's house, built of mud, an extension of the field on which it stands (71), is charmed by the conviviality of the village and reassured by its apparent stability — even as he observes the reception, or better still, the appropriation of modern technology in the village where the water-wheel gives way to the pump, doors fashioned from a whole tree by the local carpenter are replaced by mass-produced ones made of iron, the donkey is joined by the motor vehicle, and local political initiatives, such as the building of a hospital and schools, are visibly altering an antique, but not timeless, landscape.

Rather than valorize a zone between cultures, the novel questions its very possibility within a situation poisoned by colonialism. For despite a precocious facility for acquiring the knowledge provided by a European education, Mustafa Sa'eed never ceases to perceive himself as an outsider in the North, aware that the English he speaks with such astonishing fluency 'is not my language' (29). Indeed rather than signs of productive cultural dialogue, the novel, in two meticulously described interiors, offers cruel parodies of transculturation: Mustapha Sa'eed's room in England, which he calls 'a den of lethal lies' (146), is furnished with a tawdry amalgam of the artefacts from an undifferentiated Africa-Arabia (scented by sandalwood, incense, and Eastern perfumes, adorned with Persian rugs, Maghrebi brass braziers, ostrich feathers, ivory and ebony figures, drawings of the shores of the Nile and the sun setting over the Red Sea); while attached to his village home, where he had resettled after his many migrations, is an outlandish simulacrum of a wing of an English-style bourgeois house built to hoard the ghoulish mementoes of his migration, its book-lined study containing 'not a single Arab book' (137). Paradoxically then a novel which itself incorporates the narrative traditions of different cultures disposes of these genres in order to dramatize a state of permanent emergency as intrinsic to the colonial experience of modernity, divided between an affection for and a dislocation from tradition, drawn towards but not integrated into the modern as this had been received by way of an aggressive and predatory colonialism.[11]

Thus whereas the reserves and energies of a rural Islamic society in Africa are made known by the narrator, so too are the constraints and coercions of its traditions. On overhearing a bawdy conversation between the village elders, he measures his distance from their sensibilities concerning sexual relations and customary marriage norms by observing, 'I looked at them: three old men and an old women laughing awhile as they stood at the grave's edge' (85). Having begun his story by reiterating 'I am from here', and even while signalling the end of an era he now finds uncongenial, he comes to lament, 'There is no room for me here' (130). Yet despite his disorientation, the novel ends not with his flight or suicide — as may have been the case with Mustapha Sa'eed — but with an uneasy rest to his crisis. Caught in the river's currents, 'half-way between north and south (. . .) unable to continue, unable to return' (167), he solicits rescue, and after comparing his own failure to make decisions with Mustafa Sa'eed's ruthless resolution (34), he does choose, electing, as he subsequently tells his auditors, to remain with the limitations and possibilities of Sudan: 'I shall live because there are a few people I want to stay with for the longest possible time and because I have duties to discharge. It is not my concern whether or not life has meaning (. . .) I shall live by force and cunning' (168–9). There is then no victor to the debate between the voices, and no untroubled occupancy of an in-between ground. But if the incongruities that give peripheral modernities their singularity remain unresolved in the present, the narrator does allude to another time and a different condition: 'We shall pull down and we shall build, and we shall humble the sun to our will; and somehow we shall defeat poverty'. And in a gesture to the future, he lets it be known that has named his daughter Hope (113).

Samir Seikaly has noted that *Season* is situated in an identified Southern space long oppressed by an imperial North, and brings the physicality of Sudan into graphic representation.[12] To this I want to add that in transcending its social ground while preserving its overwhelming presence (Marcuse), Salih's novel retains its relationship to an actual world by mediating space and time tropologically. The location of Sudan, 'a stone's throw from the equator' (60), marks both its position on the map and its place in the Northern imagination: 'Where lies the mean? Where the middle way?' asks the narrator in protest at the denial of coevality in colonialist representation of Africans: 'Just because a man has been created on the Equator some mad people regard him as a slave, others as a god' (108). Furthermore Sudan, although long divided between a politically powerful and more affluent North, culturally Islamic and with ties to the Arab world, and an impoverished South, ethnically African, in religion Muslim, Christian or animist, rich in natural and mineral resources and regarded by the North as lacking in civilization, has been the site not only of social and economic conflict but also of cultural exchange between Arabism and Africanism.[13] These schisms and entanglements are registered in the genealogy of Mustapha Sa'eed, his mother a slave from the South, his father from a community living on the borders of Egypt: in response to one of his English lovers who is confused by his appearance, Mustafa Sa'eed replies, 'I'm like Othello — Arab-African' (38). By this Salih, in contrast to other African-Arab writers, acknowledges the 'Africanness' of his Arab protagonists.[14] (The significance of this reference to *Othello* will become apparent later on, although this and other allusions in the novel to canonical literature — *Heart of Darkness*[15] and *A Passage to India* are other instances — do not form part of my discussion.)

Geography and history then are amongst the novel's protagonists, performing roles as fact and figure. In a heat-induced delirium of confused thoughts and haphazard memories, the narrator experiences the sunburnt desert as both void and womb: by day it is 'something without value' (105), so that even while citing and reciting verse he, overwhelmed by apprehensions of 'Nothing', rages, 'This is the land of despair and poetry but there is nobody to sing' (110). With night comes deliverance, and under a 'compassionate' sky he proclaims, 'This is the land of poetry and the possible' (113). Despite which after recalling the joyful gathering of his party with other travellers and local Bedouin, he dismisses it as 'a festival to nothingness (...) A feast without meaning' (114–15). The desert landscape is thus both a physical locale and the metaphysical ground on which the Freudian alignment of the demands of the life-instincts and the magnet of nullity is rehearsed, in this anticipating the novel's bravura performance of the confluence of pleasure and death.

So too the Nile has multiple functions. Moving through the novel, as it does across the immense expanse of Sudan's sun-scorched plains, it is a real river 'but for which there would have been no beginning and no end' (69), its seasonal flooding a source of life for the villages and towns on the perimeter of the desert, and a frequent cause of death by drowning (Mustapha Sa'eed disappears during one such time). It is also a mythic waterway, a 'snake god' hungry for victims (39), a metaphor of an indifferent universe, and a chart of the route from equatorial Africa to England. Moreover the torsions of its course, which 'after flowing from south to north, suddenly turns almost at right angles and flows from west to east' before resuming 'its irrevocable journey' northwards (62, 69), are imitated by the meandering but ultimately directional narrative where the North is both desire and destiny. At the time of the novel's events the centre of an imperial world-system, the home of Sudan's colonial rulers, and the promised land for privileged and ambitious colonials, the North is the lodestar for both Mustafa Sa'eed and the narrator who move from villages in the North of Sudan to London (for Mustafa Sa'eed the journey is via Cairo) in pursuit of education and opportunity.[16]

Just as the materiality of the Sudan is infused with political, cultural and metaphysical meanings, so do the different histories and cognitive traditions of both the Arabic and the metropolitan worlds pervade the novel's consciousness of time. Condensed in the 'season' of the title are the chronological system of the Muslim Hegira[17] and the calendar of the Christian Era, both of which, sometimes cryptically, are used to contextualize important and incidental moments in the novel.[18] The term also signifies the recurrent natural cycles regulating the rhythm of agrarian life as well as episodic religious pilgrimages to the holy sites of Islam and secular sojourns in foreign lands. And it accommodates the uncharted time-zones of the experiential: travelling across the desert under a merciless sun which seems to 'remain for hours without moving' (111), the narrator endures an hallucinatory suspension of duration; travelling in the realm of the senses, Mustafa Sa'eed possesses or is possessed by 'rare moments' of ecstasy, which he recalls as 'outside the bounds of time' (153) and 'worth the whole of life' (161). However the novel does register an acute awareness of historical processes, and sometimes on the fringes, sometimes central to the narrative, is a thread of metonyms and metaphors from pre-colonial times through colonialism to independence. Together these project an anti-colonial sensibility, a post-independence disillusion and anticipations of the postcolonial 'not-yet'.

Recall of this heterogeneous past spans the Islamic civilization that flowered after the Muslim conquests in Southern Europe from the 7th century C.E. and the assaults of the Crusaders on the treasure of the Eastern world, marking the beginning of Europe's thousand-year project of invasion and culminating with modern imperialism. The titles of Mustafa Sa'eed's books are *The Cross and Gunpowder*, *The Economics of Colonialism* and *The Rape of Africa*, and when on trial in an English court for the murder of his English wife, he is visited by the sounds of imperial aggression inflicted across the ages: 'the rattle of swords in Carthage and the clatter of hooves of Allenby's horses desecrating the ground of Jerusalem' (94–5) — General Allenby being a latter-day political crusader whose armies secured the British mandate over Palestine after the European war of 1914–18. Although some allusions in the novel will be obscure to readers unacquainted with Arab histories and literatures (as they are to me), many are readily identifiable as signs of empire.[19]

The memories of imperial dominion embedded in the novel are at their keenest in the recollection of colonialist violence in Sudan: Mustafa Sa'eed, who disappears in 1956, when Sudan after a long struggle had gained an incomplete and uncertain independence, was born in 1898, the year in which Anglo-Egyptian rule, which was effectively British domination, was imposed on Sudan after Kitchener's bloody victory over the Mahdi regime at Omdurman.[20] Conscious of having inverted a subordinate Arab-African persona by taking on the role of an invader and colonizer from the South in his encounters with those Englishwomen he seduced and destroyed, Mustapha Sa'eed identifies with, while excoriating, Kitchener's insolent reprimand to the defeated and shackled Mahdi rebel, Mahmoud Wad Ahmed: '"Why have you come to my country to lay waste and plunder?"

It was the intruder who said this to the person whose land it was, and the owner of the land bowed his head and said nothing' (94). This is also a reference to the compliance of his hosts when the relatives of the dead women as well the defence counsel at his trial were at pains to exonerate him — as if bowing their heads and saying nothing. So it seems as if Mustapha Sa'eed's *ressentiment* plays itself out in accordance with Fredric Jameson's account of Nietzsche's negative category 'as the revenge of the slaves upon the masters and an ideological ruse whereby the former infect the latter with a slave mentality (...) in order to rob them of their natural vitality and aggressive, properly aristocratic insolence' (Jameson, *The Political Unconscious*, 201).

Remembrance of colonialism is more overt in the comments about the schools the rulers had opened — and which the villagers feared as 'a great evil that had come to them with the armies of occupation' (20) — the colleges established, the dams constructed[21] and the railways built, undertakings which are differently construed by Mustafa Sa'eed and the narrator. For the former, a child of colonialism and anti-colonial nationalism, and author of anti-colonialist books who while in England is reputed to have been President of the Society for the Struggle for African Freedom, their cynical purpose is foremost: 'The ships at first sailed down the Nile carrying guns not bread, and the railways were originally set up to transport troops; the schools were started so as to teach us how to say "Yes" in their language' (95). A more pragmatic response is offered by the narrator, a product of the decolonizing era who, perhaps in his guise as a *hakawati*, more certainly in his role as speaker of opposing opinion, dissembles an ignorance of colonialism's motivation:

The fact that they came to our land, I know not why, does that mean that we should poison our present and our future? Sooner or later they will leave our country (...) The railways, ships, hospitals, factories and schools will be ours and we'll speak their language, without either a sense of guilt or a sense of gratitude (49–50).

Such poise extends to his habitation of a post-independence present. Although he is contemptuous of Africa's corrupt new regimes,[22] their ignominious rulers described by him as 'smooth of face, lupine of mouth, their hands gleaming with rings of precious stones' (118), on seeing the inhabitants of his home village inaugurating cooperative ventures and exercising local democracy, he reflects: 'Are these the people who are called *peasants* in books?' (64).

Having suggested that the novel dramatizes the conflict of socialities and sensibilities within a long-colonized environment, I will now propose that its spatial and temporal locations by way of rhetorical figures construe a Southern world once locked into Empire and still in fee to the North, but also separated from its one-time masters by incommensurable pasts and aspirations. The image of a railway track 'stretching out across the desert like a rope bridge between two savage mountains, with a vast bottomless abyss between them' (54) is placed between the narrator's recall of two conversations. One is his chance encounter on a train with a retired Sudanese civil servant who remembers the arrogance of English District Commissioners living in enormous palaces 'guarded by troops', behaving like gods (53); the other is an argument between an Englishman employed by the post-independence administration and a Sudanese university teacher about colonialism's project and legacy: 'They were not angry; they said such things to each other as they laughed, a stone's throw from the Equator, with a bottomless historical chasm separating the two of them' (69).

I want to pursue this notion of an historical gulf in spite of a narrator who is at pains to remind his listeners that 'over there is like here' (48), and who in his tale juxtaposes identical scenes of sexual congress in London and a Sudanese village — 'two thighs open wide and white' (48, 164). During a lecture at the American University of Beirut in 1980, Tayeb Salih remarked: 'one of the major themes of *Season* is the East/West confrontation (. . .) I have re-defined the so-called East/West relationship as essentially one of conflict, while it had previously been treated in romantic terms'.[23] The depth of this clash surfaces in the novel's violence, which according to Mona Takieddine Amyuni has no precedent in modern Arabic literature.[24] This theme is elaborated in the mapping of the exercise of imperial force onto the extremities of eroticism, tropes of contagion being attached to both.[25] In this, the most enigmatic and disturbing dimension of the novel, the worlds of reason and the normative are interpenetrated by visitations of irrational, insensate and forbidden desire, and colonialism is reconfigured as a sexual encounter compounded of affect and hatred, ecstasy and degradation, voluptuous pleasure and violent death.

In the address to which I have referred, Salih recalled that when he came under the influence of Freud's theory of man as divided between Eros and the death-instinct, he recognized this duality from the Arab tradition, and later on in *Season* he 'tried to dramatize the polarization' (15). This 'murderous war' (161) is staged both in the fatal resistance of Hosna, Mustapha Sa'eed's widow or abandoned wife, to the lust of the elderly lecher she had been forced by her male elders to marry, and more consequentially in the psycho-metaphysical drama of sado-masochistic hunger and its appeasement. This last highly artificial performance takes place in a setting dense with signs of colonial history and colonialist fantasy. Situating himself in England as the disaffected colonial intellectual, Mustafa Sa'eed teaches economics at London University and writes his anti-colonial books; situating himself in the North as the exotic outsider, he assumes the form of colonialist fears, an enraged African-Arab libertine seeking vengeance on his masters by bewitching and debauching white women whom he designates as his prey, his pursuit recalled in the idiom of Arab battles fought long ago, his bedroom described by him as 'a theatre of war' (34). Mustafa Sa'eed romanticizes his compulsion ('I am the South that yearns for the North and the ice (...) I am a thirsty desert, a wilderness of southern desire (...) a southern thirst being dissipated in the mountain passes of history in the north' (30, 38, 42), and he exploits his lovers' delirious longing for the 'tropical climes, cruel suns and purple horizons' (30) of an undifferentiated Africa and Arabia: ' "Your tongue's as crimson as a tropic sunset (...) How marvellous your black colour is! (...) the colour of magic and mystery and obscenities" ' (139); ' "I want to have the smell of you in full—the smell of rotting leaves in the jungles of Africa, the smell of the mango and the pawpaw and tropical spices, the smell of rains in the deserts of Arabia" ' (142).

Here the extravagance of the rhetoric signifies the febrile condition of an imperial imaginary inflamed by fantasies of sensual colonial places and licentious native peoples, and to designate the novel as melodrama is not a pejorative judgement but rather an attempt to suggest that Salih's representation of the confluence of desire, violence and death in the colonial encounter, cannot be contained in conventional language.[26] Hence when explaining that his seductions had awakened the urge to self-immolation in his lovers, Mustafa Sa'eed invokes images of pollution: 'You, my lady, may not know, but you—like Carnarvon when he entered Tutankhamen's tomb—have been infected with a deadly disease which has come from you know not where and which will bring about your destruction' (39). The association of sickness and a heightened eroticism is a familiar trope of modernist literature (*The Magic Mountain*, *Death in Venice*, *The Wings of the Dove*) and it is reiterated in *Season* when the narrator laments his own secret love for Hosna as evidence that he, 'like (...) millions of others—was not immune from the germ of contagion that oozes from the body of the universe' (104). However in a novel seeped in a present consciousness of time past, the refrain of a thousand-year-old lethal disease surely alludes to Europe's long imperial history, beginning with Christian raids on the riches of the Islamic world, followed by colonialism's conquest of the South and then by the 'ferocious violence' (151) of the 1914–18 war fought amongst the capitalist nations of Europe over the spoils of overseas empire and the exercise of global power. And indeed in his confessions, Mustafa Sa'eed not only conflates the pathology of this conflict with his own perverted sexual quest, but in both an actual conversation with his interlocutor and an imagined address to the English, he attributes an infectious moral corruption to imperialism, thereby inverting the colonialist dread of defilement by colonial peoples and climes:

I saw the troops returning, filled with terror, from the war of trenches, of lice and epidemics (...) My bedroom was a spring-well of sorrow, the germ of a fatal disease. The infection had stricken these women a thousand years ago, but I had stirred up the latent depths of the disease until it had got out of control and had killed. (...)
  They imported to us the germ of the greatest European violence, as seen on the Somme and at Verdun, the like of which the world has never previously known, the germ of a deadly disease that struck them more than a thousand years ago (...) I came as an invader into your very homes: a drop of the poison which you have injected into the veins of history' (34, 95).[27]

In Mustafa Sa'eed's liaison with Jean Morris[28] a contaminated eroticism is joined to colonialist rage when in the course of their murderous sexual games the Englishwoman, who expresses her passion by insulting her lover's physical appearance, destroys, amongst other valuable objects, a rare Arabic manuscript and an antique Isfahan prayer rug, both symbols of his culture.[29] A relationship dominated by psychic humiliation and the infliction of physical pain reaches its climax when Mustafa Sa'eed in response to her entreaties and driven by his own frenzy, stabs Jean Morris, the sexually-consummated death remembered by him as a moment of ecstasy: 'The sensation that, in an instant outside the bounds of time, I have bedded the goddess of Death and gazed out upon Hell from the aperture of her eyes (...) The taste of that night stays on in my mouth, preventing me from savouring anything else' (153). This recollected scene enacts 'the terrifying convergence of pleasure and death',[30] a phrase used by Herbert Marcuse in his gloss on Freud's theories of the bond between the life-instincts and the Nirvana principle (the instincts drawn into the orbit of death), a concurrence which has entered analytic writing on eroticism as a normative rather than a depraved variety of sexual experience.

Commenting on de Sade, Georges Bataille drew attention to 'this tormenting fact: the urge towards love, pushed to its limit, is an urge toward death';[31] and elsewhere he remarked that 'Sexual pleasure has so much in common with destruction that we have named the moment of its paroxysm the "little death"', in consequence of which he continues, 'the objects suggesting sexual activity to us are always connected to some disorder'.[32] Violent death as the ultimate experience of rapture for both killer and slain is a staple of pornography, from the literary erotica of de Sade and Pauline Réage/Dominique Aury (*The Story of O*, 1954), to illiterate snuff movies/videos, where the performances take place in Nowhere, whether a remote castle or a squalid room. It has also been the subject of mainstream novels such as J.G. Ballard's *Crash* (1973), Muriel Spark's *The Driver's Seat* (1974) and Ian McEwan's *The Comfort of Strangers* (1981), as well as of the art-house Japanese film *In the Realm of the Senses* (1976), in all of which the place and the time of the narratives are either transparent or intimated—indeed *The Realm of the Senses* alludes to connections between the central couple's terminal sado-masochism and the rise of Japanese militarism and fascism,[33] while *Crash* announces itself as a cautionary tale about the libidinal excitations of the car crash which results in mutilation, genital wounds, and crippling injuries, and is apotheosized in violent death at the moment of orgasm. Within postcolonial writing, the singularity of Salih's novel, which deals with pornographic matter without being pornographic, is in its proffering an intimate nexus between erotic and colonialist extremity, joining the prodigious language of exorbitant desire pursued in private with colonial aggression displayed in public, bringing into proximity moments of deviant sexual ecstasy and acts of imperial atrocity, aligning the patently political with the opacity of the psychopathological, inflecting history with histrionics. I have hesitated to call the novel's modernist admixture of realist discourse and fantastic fabrication an allegory of empire's excess, but perhaps this is what it is.

In one of his many gnomic remarks, the narrator reflects on Mustafa Sa'eed's season of migration: 'Mustafa Sa'eed said to them, "I have come to you as a conqueror." A melodramatic phrase certainly. But their own coming too was not a tragedy as we imagine, nor yet a blessing as they imagine. It was a melodramatic act which with the passage of time will change into a mighty myth' (60). Because such linguistic obfuscation screens the substance of colonialism's history and its aftermath, the dictum could be seen to clash with the novel's embedded historical registers. But perhaps the predication is directed at inviting the reader to comprehend the colonial encounter through the non-realist genres of 'tragedy', 'melodrama' and 'myth'[34] — narrative modes which by breaking free of the empirical zone may give access to the prohibited exhilarations and irrational experiences expunged from the authorized version, and without occluding an indictment of empire's reality.

To consider this possibility, I want to return to Marcuse's thinking on the emancipatory potential of the aesthetic dimension. Drawing on both Marxist and Freudian thinking in advocating social and instinctual liberation, Marcuse argued that 'the ingression of the primary erotic-destructive forces' in 'esoteric' literature (Poe, Baudelaire, Proust, Valéry and Mallarmé), explodes 'the normal universe of communication and behaviour', and in so doing 'opens the tabooed zones of nature and society in which even death and the devil are enlisted as allies in the refusal to abide by the law and order of repression' (20–1).[35] According to Paul Robinson, Marcuse's alienation from and hostility to 'the existing intellectual and material culture' led him to entertain the oppositional force of 'the most negative and violent intellectual constructions', including 'the critical function of sexual perversion' (*The Freudian Left*, 186, 207). While this proposition on the immanent social radicalism of all transgression against a scandalous social order could be cited in praise of a novel that yokes a death-propelled eroticism to colonial violence, the consequences of bringing Marcuse's dialectical reversal to *Season* remain for me a problem. In 'Race and Gender: the Role of Analogy in Science', Nancy Stepan argued that because interactive metaphors shape our perceptions and actions while neglecting or suppressing information that does not fit the similarity, 'they tend to lose their metaphoric nature and be taken literally'.[36] On the other hand rather than perceiving the analogical turn as illegitimately aligning what is heterogeneous and distinct, we can follow Terry Eagleton in looking at allegory as 'that figurative mode which relates through difference, preserving the relative autonomy of a set of signifying units while suggesting an affinity with some other range of signifiers'.[37] Or we could consider Fredric Jameson's understanding of the 'allegorical spirit' not in terms of equivalences but as 'profoundly discontinuous, a matter of breaks and discontinuities, of the multiple polysemia of the dream rather than the homogenous representation of the symbol'.[38] Do then Salih's transfigurations of an historical colonialism expand and enhance understanding of its concealed aspects, or does the novel, by associating the imperial project with a tainted but mutual love between representatives of colonized and colonizer, attenuate and indeed distort the particularity of the colonial conflict? Since a case for both suppositions can be made, I am proposing that the 'literary' in *Season* allows new ways of seeing colonialism even as it mystifies empire's gigantic material appetites and the psychic gratifications these generated, and even as it subsumes under the erotic the political energy of colonial *ressentiment* it has animated.

BENITA PARRY

NOTES

My thanks to Laura Chrisman, Nick Harrison, Neil Lazarus, and Sabry Hafez for their comments on a draft.

1   Translated by Denys Johnson-Davies (London, Heinemann, 1969). References are to the recent Penguin edition (Harmondsworth, 2003) with an Introduction by Salih.

2   This is a field so linguistically and culturally various that critics often find themselves obliged to rely on translations and to depend on the researches of others for an understanding of the literature's social and political contexts.

3   In *Postmodernism, or the Cultural Logic of Late Capitalism*, Jameson maintains that 'Modernism must (...) be seen as uniquely corresponding to an uneven moment of social development' (London, Verso, 1991), 307. Elsewhere Jameson has proposed the provisional hypothesis 'that the possibility of magic realism as a formal mode is constitutively dependent on a type of raw material in which disjunction is structurally present; or, to generalize the hypothesis more starkly, magic realism depends on a content which betrays the overlap or the coexistence of precapitalist with nascent capitalist or technological features.' 'On Magic Realism in Film', in *Critical Inquiry* 12 (Winter 1986), 301–25; 311. In Bloch's account the return during the Nazi era to earlier forces and past levels of consciousness, was a symptom and component of a morbid condition. See 'Nonsynchronism and the Obligation to Its Dialectics' [1932], *New German Critique* 11 (Spring 1977), 22–38.

4   In colonial locations vast rural populations provided the material ground for the persistence of entrenched social practices and the survival of older psychic dispositions, towards which the colonial state strategically feigned deference. Moreover while boasting of a civilizing mission in developing

the wasted and underused material resources in the cause of international progress, elevating the minds and augmenting the rudimentary souls of the colonized, colonialism planned the retardation of the non- or nascent capitalist worlds. This is not to say that the regimes were able to control economic development, since deliberated programmes imploded under the impact of capitalism's own dynamics; nor were they able to contain the social agency of either the bourgeoisie or the populace as new modes of production generated new social relationships and altered forms of consciousness. In this connection, radical anti-colonialisms can be seen to express the determination of colonial populations to occupy fully a temporal condition into which they had been thrust by capitalism's global reach and which colonialist doctrine and practice sought to withhold.

5 See Marshall Berman, *All That Is Solid Melts Into Air: The Experience of Modernity* (London, Verso, 1982/3); Perry Anderson, 'Modernity and Revolution', *New Left Review* 144 (March–April 1984), 96–113; David Harvey, *The Condition of Postmodernity* (Oxford, Blackwell, 1989); Fredric Jameson, *Postmodernism Or The Cultural Logic of Late Capitalism* (London, Verso, 1991).

6 *The Aesthetic Dimension: Toward A Critique of Marxist Aesthetics* (London, Macmillan, 1979), 6. Marcuse is here following Adorno: 'There is no material content, no formal category of artistic creation, however mysteriously transmitted and itself unaware of the process, which did not originate in the empirical reality from which it breaks free.' 'Adorno on Brecht' in *Aesthetics and Politics* (London, New Left Books, 1977) 190. On Marcuse, see Paul A, Robinson, *The Freudian Left* (New York, Harper and Row, 1969), Fredric Jameson, *Marxism and Form* (Princeton, Princeton University Press, 1971) and Barry Katz, *Herbert Marcuse and the Art of Liberation* (London, Verso, 1982).

7 'Al-hakawati is a Syrian term for this poet, actor, comedian, historian and story-teller. Its root is *hikayah* a fable or story, or *haka*, to tell a story; wati implies expertise in a popular street-art. The *hakawati* is neither a troubadour, who travels from place to place, nor a rawi, whose recitations are more formalized and less freely interpreted. The *hakawati* has popular counterparts in Egypt, where he is often called *sha'ir*, or poet, and where he accompanies his tales on a *rababah*, a simple stringed instrument. In Iraq he is known as *qisa khoun*.' 'The Last Hakawati', http://almashriq.hiof.no/syria/700/790/the_last_hakawati/ (consulted October 2004).

8 'Sentimental Orientalism: *Season of Migration to the North* and *Othello*', in *Tayeb Salih's Season of Migration to the North: A Casebook*, edited by Mona Takieddine Amyuni (Beirut, American University of Beirut, 1985).

9 *The Political Unconscious* (London, Methuen, 1981), 201–2.

10 'The Empire Renarrated: *Season of Migration to the North* and the Reinvention of the Present', in Patrick Williams and Laura Chrisman, *Colonial Discourse and Post-Colonial Theory: A Reader* (Hemel Hempstead, Harvester Press, 1993), 537.

11   If peripheral modernities did not register an absolute break with the past, this does not imply a nativist or regressive position on the modern, but rather a politically-motivated recollection of histories insulted by the colonialist and directed at furthering a wider anti-colonial consciousness and awakening anticipations of a postcolonial future. Moreover while the new technologies were embraced for their potential to liberate labour from physical servitude and free humankind of scarcity, the ethos of the technologically innovative oppressors was often refused.

12   'Season of Migration to the North: History in the Novel', in Amyuni.

13   See *The Southern Sudan: The Problem of National Integration*, edited by Dunstan M. Wai (London, Frank Cass, 1973) and *The African-Arab Conflict in the Sudan*, edited by Dunstan M. Wai (New York and London, Africana, 1981).

14   As Anouar Majid writes in a chapter entitled 'The North as Apocalypse': 'A dominant motif of canonical postcolonial works by Africans of Muslim descent is the young educated protagonist's wrenching deracination from his or her indigenous culture, followed by catastrophic, even suicidal, journeys to the Northern metropoles'. See *Unveiling Traditions: Postcolonial Islam in a Polycentric World* (Durham and London, Duke University Press, 2000), 78.

15   See M. Peeled, 'Portrait of an Intellectual', *Journal of Middle Eastern Studies* (May 1977), 218–28, and Gayatri Chakravorty Spivak, who in *Death of a Discipline* (New York, Columbia University Press, 2003) interprets *Season* as a transgressive reading of Conrad.

16   Anouar Majid refers to Cheikh Hamidou Kane's *Ambiguous Adventure* and Ken Bugul's *The Abandoned Baobab* as well as *Season*.

17   A footnote tells us this began in 622 Christian Era. Edward Said refers to the voyages narrated by the novel as being converted into a 'sacralized *hegira* from the Sudanese countryside (...) into the heart of Europe', *Culture and Imperialism* (London, Chatto and Windus, 1995), 255.

18   There are references to the journey taken by the narrator's grandfather to Egypt in 1306 of the Muslim calendar (1928 C.E) and the lives of the two narrators are meticulously measured out in spans of years: the first narrator spends 7 years of study in England, returning at age 25; Mustafa Sa'eed's migration to the North lasts for 30 years, his imprisonment for 7 years and his stay in the village 5 years. The precise significance of the numerated years in which seven recurs, is not apparent to me but would no doubt be of interest to those who attribute metaphysical or magical properties to particular numbers. Note too the repetition of the thousand years of European aggression.

19   While scanning an old issue of *The Times* of 1927 the narrator sees mention of 'Kenya Colony', of a dispute between Muslims and Hindus in the Punjab, and of the Treaty of Jeddah 'signed by Sir Gilbert Clayton on behalf of Great Britain and Prince Feisal Abdul Aziz Al Saud', 150.

20   This was in revenge at the death of General Gordon at Khartoum during the Mahdi uprising of 1885, which had overthrown Anglo-Egyptian rule.

Contemporary historians regard the Mahdi as an early form of anti-colonial nationalism. 'As the Knight of Empire, Sir Herbert Kitchener, made final preparations to advance, against the flow of the river, upon the town that would soon be looted and burnt to honour his victory, Mustafa Sa'eed was born in one of its dark and apprehensive alleys (...) It is around this bloody encounter and its aftermath, between an independent theocratic Sudan and an insatiable British empire, between (...) a messianic Islam and a missionary Christianity, that the entire destiny of Mustafa Sa'eed revolves.' Samir Seikaly in Amyuni, 136.

21   On page 54 is a reference to the Senna Dam, which according to Basil Davidson, a severe critic of British Empire in Africa, is the one great success story of colonialism, and the one exception to the many schemes that were implemented to serve the needs of the colonial regimes. Built in 1925 under the British administration it dramatically improved life for the inhabitants of the Gezara region and was expanded by an independent Sudan in 1965.

22   And indeed the novel juxtaposes the grandiose plans for Africa's future being devised in ostentatious buildings, with the popular schemes implemented at a local level in cooperative ventures. This gap between the countryside and the modernized capital city Khartoum is imaged in the contrast of a dancing circle spontaneously formed in the desert by Bedouins and the narrator's crew on a journey north, and the Independence Hall in Khartoum 'an imposing edifice (...) constructed in the form of a complete circle', designed in London, using white marble imported from Italy and costing more than a million pounds (119).

23   Address to American University of Beirut, 18 May 1980, in Amyuni, 15.

24   Preface to Amyuni.

25   There are perhaps affinities with Assia Djebar's *Fantasia: An Algerian Cavalcade* (1985), translated by Dorothy Blair (London, Quartet, 1989), which alternates impressionistic recuperations of the French invaders 'coming as lovers' to Algeria (2), with the record of their brutality: 'the silence of this majestic mourning is but the prelude to the cavalcade of screams and carnage which fill the ensuring decades', and whose narrator is 'haunted by the agitation of the killers, by their obsessive unease' (57). 'My writing is immediately caught in the snare of the old war between two peoples. So I swing like a pendulum from images of war (a war of conquest and liberation but a war in the past) to the expression of a contradictory and ambiguous love' (216).

26   See Richard Murphy, *Theorizing the Avant-Garde* (Cambridge, Cambridge University Press, 1998), especially the chapter on 'Expressionist Drama and the Melodramatic Imagination'.

27   A minor character Mansour says to an Englishman employed by the Ministry of Finance in independent Sudan: 'You transmitted to us the disease of your capitalist economy' (60).

28 Jareer Abu-Haydar, 'A Novel Difficult to Categorise', in Amyuni. Abu-Haydar refers to Salih's close friendship with the Palestinian poet Tawfiq Sayigh whose sadomasochistic love affair with English women is transfigured in his verse.

29 Sabry Hafez pointed this out to me. Interestingly the cover photograph of the new Penguin edition displays not these items but the expensive Wedgwood vase, which Jean Morris also smashes, juxtaposed with a fabric of indeterminate floral design.

30 *Eros and Civilization: A Philosophical Inquiry into Freud* (1955) (New York, Vintage Books, 1962), 23, 24.

31 *Eroticism* (London, Marion Boyars, 1962), 42.

32 *The Absence of Myth: Writings on Surrealism*, translated by Michael Richardson (London, Verso, 1994), 203.

33 Pointed out to me by Laura Chrisman.

34 Suggested to me by Nick Harrison.

35 Consider also Marcuse's comment on writings inspired by the horror of fascism (Brecht, Sartre, Günter Grass and Paul Celan): 'the transforming mimesis terminates in the recognition of the infamous reality of fascism (. . .) And this recognition is a triumph: in the aesthetic form (of the play, the poem, the novel), the terror is called up, called by its name, and made to testify, to denounce itself (. . .) By virtue of this achievement of mimesis, these works contain the quality of Beauty in its perhaps most sublimated form: as political Eros. In the creation of an aesthetic form (. . .) the life-instincts rebel against the global sado-masochistic phase of contemporary civilization' (64).

36 In *Anatomy of Race*, edited by David Theo Goldberg (Minneapolis, University of Minnesota Press, 1990), 52.

37 Terry Eagleton, *The Significance of Theory* (Oxford, Blackwell, 1990), 58.

38 'Third World Literature in the Era of Multinational Capitalism', *Social Text* 15 (1986), 65–87, 73.

Literary Misunderstanding

The first misunderstanding may well concern the very notion of misunderstanding. Indeed anyone who consults a dictionary will notice a strange discrepancy between the meaning of the notion set out in the dictionary definitions and the meaning that emerges from the various citations.

The *Trésor de la langue française* states two meanings of the term as follows: 'a divergence of interpretation regarding the meaning of words or acts leading to disagreement; a disagreement brought about by such a divergence'.[1] The definition is clear and draws upon a world of familiar experience in which misunderstandings are perceived as a matter of erroneous interpretation that can be traced readily to some ambivalence in the signs to be interpreted. 'It is just a misunderstanding', as they say.

In these terms misunderstanding appears to be the most benign form of the difficulty of understanding and understanding one another. It is often thought that this derives from the absence of a precise list of signs and their respective meanings. So we like to dream of a form of communication, devoid of misunderstandings, that would result from a language that defined its object unequivocally. We also like to think that evil spirits thwart the use of this language and capitalize on misunderstandings: all kinds of deception are inflicted on us in this way, via the manipulation of words and attitudes with double meanings that lead us to perceive the opposite of what we should. But the same also applies to those who make their living from words whose very value depends on their inaccessibility; those who employ obscure words to disguise the banality of what they have to say, and who, as soon as you presume to challenge them on what you have understood — that is, something banal — retort that there has been a misunderstanding.

Thus misunderstanding appears well circumscribed and the notion, if we believe the *Trésor de la langue française*, has been fixed since the sixteenth century and thus coincides with the stabilization of the French language. How then can we explain the strange examples cited in the same article to illustrate this business of language ill-understood? I quote: Jankelevitch: 'It is the trickery of love which gives rise to the most serious misunderstandings'. Martin du Gard: 'At the root of all passionate love there is, inevitably, a misunderstanding, a generous illusion, an error of judgement, a misconception of the one by the other.' And Zola on the unhappy marriage of the engineer Hennebeau in *Germinal*: 'Their discord had grown, aggravated by one of those strange misunderstandings of the flesh which can freeze the warmest heart: he adored his wife, and she had all the sensuality of a voluptuous blonde, but already they slept apart, ill at ease with each other, quick to take offence.'[2] Here it can no longer be said that the misunderstanding has occurred simply because one of the partners has misinterpreted the attitudes or speech of the other. The misunderstanding is between two fleshes. This is not merely a euphemism to indicate the incapacity of a male organ to respond to the sensual provocations of a voluptuous blonde. More radically than this, Zola's sentences suggest an essential link between the failure of relations between two bodies and the capacity for playing with the words 'the sensuality of a voluptuous blonde', an essential connection between the felicity of the phrase and the impenetrability of the bodies, between the power of speech and the lack at the heart of the 'sexual relation'.

The dictionary does not bother to note — let alone explain — this discrepancy between two misunderstandings, between a simple matter of badly read signs and a non-relation constitutive of the very capacity to emit and interpret signs. The misunderstanding of misunder-standings finds its home in precisely that shady zone separating the dreamed-of list of words' meanings from that specific form of usage in which the felicity of the words serves to speak the suffering of bodies: literature. Not that the *Trésor de la langue française* fails to invoke literature as an example of misunderstanding. But it is there in a form that offers a peculiarly restricted understanding of literary activity. If Zola stages a lack at the very heart of the relation between language and sexuation, a commonplace borrowed from Thibaudet refers literary misunderstandings back to a less offensive common-place: 'misunderstanding and hostility between artists and society cannot be denied.'

The fact remains that this cliché is still an enigma. Neither Thibaudet's sentence nor the dictionary definition helps us to grasp why misunderstanding and hostility are taken as synonymous or why he has chosen to term the familiar spectacle of mutual incomprehen-sion between artists and grocers 'misunderstanding'. It is true that the matter has been discussed at length elsewhere. But this has been at the expense of turning misunderstanding into a sham. I am thinking of course in particular of the famous passages from *What is Literature?* where Sartre tries to define the status of literature in the era which, according to him, begins with the clash of June 1848: 'Indeed, from

1848 on (...) it was taken for granted that it was better to be unrecognized than famous, that success — if the writer ever achieved it in his lifetime — was to be explained by a misunderstanding.'[3]

Sartre defines misunderstanding as the feature of an epoch, the epoch of literature, in which literature asserted itself as literature through a number of paradigmatic figures: Baudelaire, Flaubert, Mallarmé, Rimbaud, Proust... But he defines it in a very singular way that is at once both minimal in its content and radical in its form.

Radical in its form: authors do not want to be understood. They refuse to serve the ends assigned to literature by a bourgeois public. For good measure they refuse to serve any ends at all, beyond those of art itself.

Minimal in its content: the argument about misunderstanding does not refer back to any structural specificity through which the work might evade comprehension. The idea of the misunderstanding is merely postulated and is a corollary of translating the attitude of writers who assume on principle that even when they have been admired it has not been for the real reasons that make them admirable.

This 'misunderstanding' is therefore perfectly well understood. Artists, as portrayed by Sartre, strive not to be understood, to say the minimum possible, to say nothing. Not serving the ends of the bourgeois oppressor (*les fusilleurs*) is also a way of establishing a certain distance, which helps artists affirm their identity and by which the artistic elite distinguishes itself from the vulgar masses.[4] This suits everybody: the artists, who are pleased that the *fusilleurs* are defending their assets; and the *fusilleurs*, who fear nothing so much as a literature that might reveal to their victims the real state of the world and their subordination within in.

By this account, the misunderstanding appears to be fictitious. It would be the fiction that seals the tacit contract between the literary elite and the socio-political elite at the expense of the public, that is, in the final analysis, the people. This presumes that the elite is in agreement about its actions. Yet any such agreement is far from apparent. Indeed, it would seem that those closest to each other do not at all agree about what they are doing. Here for example is a letter addressed to a writer by a very close friend about other close friends. Flaubert writes to George Sand:

You talk of 'my friends', you talk of 'my school'. (...) The writers I often see, and those whom you mention, all cherish the things I scorn and care very little for the things that haunt me. (...) Goncourt, for instance, is so pleased when he has picked up a word in the street that he can paste into a book, whereas I am contented if I have written a page without assonances or repetitions.[5]

It is no longer a question here of a misunderstanding advanced in order to protect the elite soul from any risk of being understood by the vulgar masses. The failure of communication occurs precisely between those writers who make up the elite. Talking about misunderstanding is a way of discussing the very texture of the book in particular and the 'literary' more generally. These misunderstandings are not about what one group or another 'means to say'. They are about what writers do in the very passages describing characters or situations devoid of any enigmatic quality.

Take another example: the misunderstanding that pits Henri Ghéon and Proust against each other with regard to the description of the church at Combray. Ghéon bemoans the overload of detail: 'M. Proust will not even spare us Mme Sazerat with her little box of cakes; it is enough for him to remember having seen her once in church!'[6]

Proust's response is well known:

You think that I mention Madame Sazerat because I don't dare omit that I saw her that day. But I never saw her (. . .) By placing end to end the little impressions I experienced during the impassioned and lucid hours I was able to spend over the course of various years at the *Sainte-Chapelle*, Pont-Audemer, Caen and Evreux I have pieced together the stained-glass window. I placed Madame Sazerat in front of it in order to enhance the human feel of the church at such-and-such an hour. But all my characters and all the circumstances of my book are invented with a particular meaning in mind (*dans un but de signification*).[7]

Thus the misunderstanding bears neither on a linguistic ambiguity or obscurity, nor on an enigma to interpret. Ghéon is not even bemoaning the length of Proust's sentences. And Madame Sazerat has no symbolic significance. The misunderstanding is not hermeneutic, in its habitual sense. It concerns a trivial matter: the status to be accorded to the presence of an individual on a kneeler. Thus, all in all, the misunderstanding is, in the strict sense of the word, a miscalculation (*mécompte*), a falling-out over an account (*compte*). For Ghéon, there is a being too many in that scene. But his critique of this being-too-many stems from a misunderstanding of this particular being-there.

Let's be clear. Ghéon is not naïve. He is not the victim of the disdain of Don Quixote before the puppets of Master Peter. Nor does he believe, like the Duc de Guermantes, that novelists go around salons with nets in which to catch the people they meet there. He knows that Madame de Sazerat is a fictional character. And this is precisely why he sees her as superfluous in this scene. Fictional characters have a number of traits that distinguish them from real-life beings. Authors are not obliged to depict them in every chance encounter and with all the particular characteristics that pertain to the concrete existence of real individuals. Encounters and characteristics should be pared down to what is useful to fiction.

This is precisely the mistake Proust makes. He is the one who confuses reality and fiction. There is no fictional need to name the character on whom a ray of light refracted by the window falls — especially if her name is Madame Sazerat, a character known to the reader only as the presumed owner of an unidentified dog. Thus the critic is bound to conclude: if this character, whose presence is fictionally inconsequential and who could be substituted for any other, is there on the kneeler, it is because she was already there, because the author did not know how to withdraw her from a composition shaped not by any novelistic necessity but by his own memories.

The novelist's failing is therefore the complete opposite of the one articulated in Sartre's critique. Sartre highlighted the taste for rarefaction, for holding back, the nihilistic desire to say nothing (*rien dire*). Whereas Proust's failing seems rather to be his inability to hold anything back, to prevent himself from saying everything. But to say everything (*tout dire*) is to be unaware of the sort of '(every)thing' that a work of art constitutes, that is, an organic individual, possessed of all the constituent parts necessary for life and nothing more.

As for that organic satisfaction we get from a work where we take in all its parts, its form at a glance, he stubbornly declines to provide it. The time that anyone else would have used to let a little light into this dense forest, to open up spaces in it and provide vistas, he gives to counting the trees, the various kinds of species, the leaves on the ground. And he will describe every leaf in the way it differs from the others, vein by vein, front and back. That is his delight and his affectation. He writes 'pieces' (*morceaux*). (Ghéon, 'Review of *Swann*', 106)

Proust's miscalculation thus creates an opposition between two ideas of the whole. On the one hand the 'animal', endowed with all the required limbs, assembled in the unity of a form. On the other hand, the 'vegetable' infinity, an endlessly fragmented totality. And the critic is assigning a social aetiology to this latter pathology of writing; if the writer gets lost in the detail, it is because he is a 'gentleman of leisure'. He has all the time in the world to create his 'pieces', because he has all the time in the world to look at stained-glass windows, to wander through the world, to observe people and so on, because he shares in the time of the privileged.

Proust, as we know, dismantles this argument point by point. Literature for him is the complete opposite of a 'stock list of sensations and the inventory of his knowledge' (Ghéon 106). There is not a single excess body in his book. Everything therein has been invented to serve the purpose of a fiction that must demonstrate an idea. Finally, he has no leisure. He is not a dilettante who hangs around in salons and takes home sketches, but an invalid, shut away, for whom the clock is ticking. This response is not simply a personal justification. Broadly taken, it expresses the misunderstanding about literature. Proust was not the first to have heard the argument about the 'living creature' (*bel animal*) broken up into a heap of bodies.[8] The criticism had already resounded in the ears of writers who were not all of the same filiation: Hugo, Balzac, Zola, Flaubert and others. The same reproach was made to all those writers who invented this new form of the art of writing that we call literature: incapable of leaving things out, they would impede the individuality of the whole by weighing it down with ever more detail. Listen for example to Pontmartin commenting on *Madame Bovary*: 'A hideous villager wants to be bled: description of the dish, the arm, the shirt, the lancet, the spurt of blood. Monsieur Homais, the *bel esprit* pharmacist, buys some little cakes in Rouen: description of the little cakes (...) A beggar holds out his hands beside a main road: description (...).'[9]

The argument relates to literature as such, and not to the lifestyle of this or that writer. It is about a politics of literature. At the heart of this politics is the relationship between saying everything and a certain political and social state. Ghéon interprets this relationship in the bluntest of terms: if you do not stop, it is because you do not have to, because you are privileged and have time. Pontmartin, as a good reactionary, goes to the heart of the matter. The problem for him is not the time that writers may or may not possess in accordance with their wealth; it is the symbolic space of the coexistence of bodies. The new novel falls short of the unified totality because it expresses a structuring of this space that does not leave room to remove obstacles to the totality. Conversely the traditional novel benefited from the space created by a clearly stratified social hierarchy:

The character embodying all the refinements of birth, education and the heart left no room for secondary figures, still less for material objects. This exquisite world saw ordinary people only through the doors of its carriages and the countryside only through the windows of its palaces. This left wide and fertile scope for the analysis of the finest sentiments, which are always more complicated and harder to decipher in the souls of the elite than amongst the lower classes. (Pontmartin, 321–2)

In this sense, Flaubert is the archetypal writer of a time where everything exists on the same level and where everything must be described. A tide of beings and things, a tide of superfluous bodies floods the novel. This tide has a political name. It is called democracy. And in this sense, Proust's novel is democratic, as is Flaubert's. There are two social regimes that produce two regimes of writing. In this sense, the murky forest bemoaned by Ghéon is the effect of a new form of social vegetation. As Taine taught us, there are two main types of society corresponding to two types of tree-filled space: on the one hand the old-style arrangement of parks with grand vistas and majestic trees. On the other hand the modern jumble of shrubs squashed up against each other, suffocating, and preventing the air from circulating and the onlooker from gaining an overview. The novels of both Flaubert and Proust bear witness to this new regime of society and of writing, this indistinction of places and times called democracy.

We know that Flaubert, like Proust, had a response to this. If he chooses to count all the leaves it is not because he is a democrat, but quite the opposite, it is because, since they are all different, the leaves refute democratic uniformity. On a more profound level, the literary population requires an altogether different unit of accounting from the democratic population, a different form of individuality which is no longer molar but molecular. 'Human' individualities, defined as the unity of a body animated by a soul which determines its overall form and its particular expressions and postures, are replaced by pre-human individualities, resulting from the arbitrary mingling of atoms: encounters between a blade of grass, a swirl of dust in the air, the flash of a fingernail, a ray of sunshine, the elements which, in daily life and in the tradition of artistic representation, translate into the feelings and opinions of individuals.

In evoking the Flaubertian response to the question of the leaves, my intention has not been to add a further twist to the misunderstanding about misunderstanding, but rather to try to get to the heart of the miscalculation. The issue is not a hermeneutic one. The literary miscount is not a matter of linguistic ambiguity. It is about bodies and counting and the relation between the body count (*le compte des corps*) and the tally of words and meanings. Anti-democratic pamphleteers would like to reduce the matter to a question of population density: too many equal bodies all tumbling inexorably into the novel's net. But the excess is not numeric. It is defined in relation to a supposed harmony between the body count and the tally of words and their meanings. We should not be comparing the social density of bodies with their density in the novel. Rather, we must compare the orderliness or disorderliness of the relationship — between bodies and words — that governs two forms of fiction, the political and the literary.

Literature is concerned with democracy not in terms of the 'rule of the masses' but as an excess in the relation between bodies and words. Democracy means firstly the invention of words by means of which those who do not count make themselves count and which blur the assigned distribution of speech and silence that constitutes the community as 'living creature' or organic whole. Democratic miscalculation (*le mécompte démocratique*) consists of putting into circulation beings superfluous to any functional accounting of bodies; for example, when Blanqui gave his profession as 'proletarian' to a magistrate. This empty word, devoid of any referent, conjures a political space, a space of fictional bodies surpassing any structured account of social bodies, of their places and functions. The excess does not stem from the large numbers invoked, but rather from the account's doubling-up (*dédoublement du compte*). For it consists of the introduction of an account undoing the close fit of bodies to meanings.

This is where political disagreement (*la mésentente politique*) comes in.[10] This is also where we can weigh up the relationship between politics and literature and between political disagreement and literary 'misunderstanding'. The latter operates to the detriment of the same structuring paradigm as the former, that is, the 'living creature' (*bel animal*), composed as a harmony of limbs and functions in an organic whole. The model of the 'living creature' is also a paradigm for the ideal proportionate relation between bodies and meanings, a paradigm of correspondence and saturation: in any given community there should be no names-of-bodies circulating in excess of real bodies, no floating or supernumerary names, liable to create new fictions and thereby to divide the whole, undoing its form and functionality. No more than there should in a poem be bodies superfluous to the requirements of arrangements of meanings, no state of body unlinked by a clear expressive relation to a state of meaning.

Both political disagreement and literary misunderstanding thus undermine an aspect of the consensual paradigm of the ideal proportion between words and things. Disagreement invents words, statements, arguments and proofs that forge new groups in which anyone can stand up and be counted in the tally of the uncounted. Misunderstanding works away at relations and accounts from another angle, by suspending the forms of individuality by which consensual logic binds bodies to meanings. Politics works on the whole, literature works on individual units. Its particular form of dissensuality (*dissensualité*) consists of creating new forms of individuality which undo established links between states of body and meaning, 'leaves' which conceal the tree from its owner. It is the same with the little cakes on Madame Sazerat's kneeler — and even more so the hazy flock of seagulls on the shore at Balbec. Ditto the *cheminots* bought by Monsieur Homais in Rouen[11] — and even more so the tall slender grass, the little blue bubbles on the wavelets, the fine-legged insects and the rays of sunshine whose combined effect can be translated under the old heading: 'Emma's love for Léon'.[12]

This argument has two implications, one peculiar to literary dissensus, the other concerning its relation to political dissensus. The first implication concerns the relationship between disconnected units and the whole. It seems evident that the form inhabited by these individualities is incompatible with the shape of the 'living creature' or the park with the grand vistas and majestic trees. But this does not exclude all notion of the whole. Indeed, on the contrary, a whole becomes necessary, not in order to limit the count but rather to authenticate the individualities, to reveal them as manifestations of the same substance. If this were not the case then Madame Sazerat's little cakes or Monsieur Homais's *cheminots* would indeed remain childhood memories pasted into the books. If the whole is not to be the sum of all its parts then it must instead be the substance immanent in its units. But how does this immanence manifest itself? Perhaps the substance of literature is condemned to prove itself only by means of miscalculations, by procedures of subtraction or addition.

The first form is the one embraced by Flaubert in the letter to George Sand cited above; the practice of the word picked up in the street and pasted into the book is countered by the work that eventually generates a page 'without assonances or repetitions'. Conceived in these terms, the page will create, in its own way, the characteristics of the absent 'living creature'; no more and no less than what is strictly necessary, nothing more than the leaves and the wind that moves them together, turning them into the perceptible form of the wind's changes. The page should make this understood rather than seen (*non pas voir mais entendre*), substituting the concept-free immediacy of the Idea for the notion of the whole. But no page will ever reveal this consubstantiality of wind and leaves. The work of elimination only promises it at the risk of eventually rendering the music of the Idea indistinguishable from the prose of the world.

The second form is the one Proust adopts: the whole must come as something extra, in the form of self-affirmation. 'All my characters and all the circumstances of my book are invented with a particular meaning in mind.' He says it here in a letter, but he must also say it in the book itself, in this book that nevertheless excludes 'theories' and declarations of authorial intent. His response thus presents itself as a performative contradiction. In literature intentions do not count. If authors have to say what they have done, then they have failed to do it.

This means too that the individuality of the whole that unites literary individualities can never be consubstantial with these individualities themselves. The Proustian novel as a whole is condemned to be a 'living creature', a story with a beginning, a middle and an end, a tale of illusion and recognition in which every episode is directed towards that recognition. Even if it means that the end — that is to say, the general rule as lived, as constituted by individualities — disrupts the scenario of totalization, by making it known that individualities — that is, truths — exist as such only when they are not sought out, not constructed, but allowed to impose themselves, like the veins of the leaf on the stone. It follows that no body on any kneeler will ever be able to shake off the suspicion of being a being-too-many. In this sense misunderstanding is indeed the rule of literature and not simply the procedure behind the vicissitudes of its unstable reception or its pre-ordained non-reception.

The second implication is the divergence of political disagreement and literary misunderstanding. Literary dissensus concerns shifts in scale and in the nature of individualities and the deconstruction of relationships between states of things and meanings. In this way it does more than differentiate itself from the work of political subject-formation, which through words configures new groupings of people. In contrast to the scene of speech peculiar to political disagreement it tends to set up another scene of other relations between meanings and states of being which come to shake the foundations of political subject-formation. This other scene is a double scene of silent utterance (*parole muette*): on the one hand, the scene of those things that speak the shared universe better than any political rhetoric, that speak better than any orator, just as long as you unravel the hieroglyphics of shared history inscribed on their bodies. On the other hand, the scene of those silent things that serve no purpose, bear no meaning and draw consciences into their apathy and aphasia. This is the universe of less than human micro-individualities, which demand a very different scale from that imposed by political subjects. Literary dissensus inaugurates both a scene of super-significance and sub-significance. And in the gap between the two it seems forever doubtful that literature might ever be able to offer the guarantee of goodwill sometimes demanded of it: namely of capturing worldly experience in such a way as to help configure a shared universe of political debate, judgement and action. Literary misunderstanding thus tends to remove itself from the service of political disagreement. It has its own politics, or rather metapolitics. On the one hand literature reads the signs written on bodies, on the other it releases bodies from the meanings they are expected to shoulder.

Literature, it is true, does claim to offer us other services in exchange for those it withholds. It claims to cure us of certain miscalculations, and in particular of the miscalculation that assembles a multiplicity of bodily states — a coloured stain moving on a beach or a ray of sunshine on a drop of water or a swirl of dust — into the whole of an individualized body and then attributes the meaning 'love' to this totalized body in which we totalize ourselves.

This brings us back to the dictionaries with which we began. It is no coincidence if the 'misunderstandings of the flesh' are immediately taken to illustrate differences of interpretation with regard to acts or speech. Literature teaches us to choose between two interpretations: not two interpretations of the speech or actions of others, but two interpretations of our own perceptions and the feelings of affection that accompany them. There is the interpretation that converts into individual figures the shifting outlines of the moving stain and from these figures isolates the love object to be possessed. And there is the interpretation that converts them into metaphorical elements to be thrown on to the big wheel of metaphors of writing.[13] This is where fiction and 'real life' go their separate ways, contrary to popular belief. This is also where we get to the heart of the misunderstanding. It is what Ghéon fails to recognize when he argues that things from real life do not belong in fiction. He cannot grasp that literature is the real life that heals us from the misunderstandings of both the fictions of love and the fictions of politics. The misunderstanding that literature sustains is the price to pay for the cure it offers from other misunderstandings.

Thus literature teaches us to do what the lexicographer may not, that is, to choose our misunderstandings carefully.

JACQUES RANCIÈRE

(Translated by Mary Stevens)

NOTES

1　*Trésor de la langue française* (Paris, Gallimard, 1985), volume XI, 250.
2　Adapted from Emile Zola, *Germinal*, translated by Peter Collier (Oxford, Oxford University Press, 1993), 201.
3　Adapted from Jean-Paul Sartre, 'What is Literature?' in *'What is Literature?' and Other Essays*, translated by Bernard Frechtman (Cambridge, Massachussetts, Harvard University Press, 1988), 109.
4　Translator's note: in speaking of the *les fusilleurs* (literally, 'members of a firing squad') Sartre is making a specific reference to those members of the ruling classes who contributed to the violent suppression of the workers' revolt of June 1848 and to the Paris Commune in 1871. See 'What is Literature?', 121–2.
5　Adapted from Gustave Flaubert, 'To George Sand, late December 1875' in *Selected Letters*, translated by Geoffrey Wall (London, Penguin, 1997), 401.
6　Henri Ghéon, 'Review of *Swann*' in the *Nouvelle Revue française* 1/1/1914, reprinted in *Marcel Proust: The Critical Heritage*, edited and translated by Leighton Hodson (London, Routledge, 1989), 107.
7　Marcel Proust, 'Letter to Henri Ghéon', 2/1/1914 in *Correspondance* (Paris, Gallimard, 1993) volume XIII, 29. Translator's note: Extracts from this letter, including part of the above quotation, appear in Jean-Yves Tadié, *Marcel Proust*, translated by Euan Cameron (London, Viking, 2000), 610–11.
8　Translator's note: the idea of the 'living creature' (*bel animal*) refers to the Platonic notion of the soul as a winged horse, housed in an earthly frame, as described in *Phaedrus*. Plato's 'living creature' was picked up as a metaphor for poetic form by Aristotle and was revived in France in the classical period. When Ghéon considers Proust's refusal to provide 'organic satisfaction' he is therefore also referring to his divergence from the Platonic model (see above).
9　Armand de Pontmartin, 'Le Roman bourgeois et le roman démocratique. MM. Edmond About et Gustave Flaubert', *Nouvelles causeries du Samedi* (Paris, Michel-Lévy, 1860), 323.
10　See Jacques Rancière, *La Mésentente. Politique et philosophie* (Paris, Galilée, 1995). English translation by Julie Rose, *Disagreement: Politics and Philosophy* (Minneapolis, University of Minnesota Press, 1998).
11　Translator's note: 'Madame Homais was very fond of these small heavy loaves, shaped like a turban, which are eaten with salt butter during Lent.' Gustave

Flaubert, *Madame Bovary*, translated by Alan Russell (London, Penguin, 1950), 310.

12   See *Madame Bovary*, 107.

13   Translator's note: for a lengthier discussion of the analogy of the big wheel to describe the play of metaphors in Proust, see Jacques Rancière, *La Parole muette* (Paris, Hachette, 1998), 158.

The original version of this essay, 'Le Malentendu littéraire', was published in *Le Malentendu: Généalogie du geste herméneutique*, edited by Bruno Clément and Marc Escola (Paris, Presses Universitaires de Vincennes, 2003), 121–32.

A Defence of Tautology: Repetition and Difference in Wordsworth's Note to 'The Thorn'

Repetition and resemblance are different in kind — extremely so.

Gilles Deleuze, *Difference and Repetition* (1968)[1]

i

When Wordsworth presented 'The Thorn' to the public for the second time, he appended a note to the poem, at the end of volume I of the 1800 *Lyrical Ballads*. Like the 'Advertisement' included in the 1798 edition, the note alerts the reader to the difference between 'the character of the loquacious narrator' of 'The Thorn' and 'the author's own person':[2] this distinction, it explains, 'ought to have been' laid out in 'an introductory poem' which, it is acknowledged, 'is necessary to give this Poem its full effect'.[3] In the absence of this preliminary verse Wordsworth offers a prose sketch of the character of the narrator, developing the hint 'so elaborately that he creates a fiction supplementary to the poem':[4]

The Reader will perhaps have a general notion of [this character], if he has ever known a man, a Captain of a small trading vessel for example, who being past the middle age of life, had retired upon an annuity or small independent income to some village or country town of which he was not a native, or in which he had not been accustomed to live. (*LB*, 350–1)

As well as standing in for the unwritten proem, the note ventures 'to add a few words closely connected with "The Thorn"', in defence of a key rhetorical principle operating in this 'and many other Poems in these volumes':

There is a numerous class of Readers who imagine that the same words cannot be repeated without tautology: this is a great error: virtual tautology is much oftener produced by using different words when the meaning is exactly the same. Words, a Poet's words more particularly, ought to be weighed in the balance of feeling, and not measured by the space which they occupy upon paper. For the Reader cannot be too often reminded that Poetry is passion: it is the history or science of feelings; now every man must know that an attempt is rarely made to communicate impassioned feelings without something of an accompanying consciousness of the inadequateness of our own powers or the deficiencies of language. During such efforts there will be a craving in the mind, and as long as it is unsatisfied the speaker will cling to the same words, or words of the same character. (*LB*, 351)

The tautology arising from reiteration of 'the same words' is differentiated from the redundancy or replication proceeding from the paraphrastic practice of 'using different words when the meaning is exactly the same'. The privileging of pure repetition implicit in this distinction is reinforced when other instances from Wordsworth's critical writings are recalled, demonstrating a lack of sympathy with paraphrastic, or periphrastic, substitution.[5] No sooner is this hierarchical opposition established, however, than it is collapsed by the tautologous energy of Wordsworth's prose. Invoking a formula expressive of infinite reiteration ('the Reader cannot be too often reminded'), the motivation for poetic repetition is emphatically identified in the axiom 'Poetry is passion', but the return of the phrase upon itself immediately introduces a critical difference, refiguring poetry as 'the history or science of feeling'.

The reformulation enacted here in a sentence is repeated on a larger scale by the note itself, which presents a 'history or science' of the 'passion' embodied in the poetry of 'The Thorn'. By appending an explanatory prose annotation to the poem, Wordsworth runs the risk of appearing to admit that 'inadequateness' or a helpless sense of the 'deficiencies of language' in the attempt 'to communicate impassioned feelings' is not limited to the protagonists of his tale, but extends to the poet himself, and that repetitive language is not so much a dramatic or rhetorical device as a symptom of a stylistic lack requiring supplementation and augmentation by the paraphrase that he purports to denigrate. The paradox inherent in this interplay of iteration and substitution is a notable feature of one influential strand of eighteenth-century literary historicism: the economy of repetition and difference structuring the poetics of *Lyrical Ballads* can, I wish later to suggest, be traced through an account of the origin of literary tropes with which Wordsworth was demonstrably familiar.

The defence of tautology embedded in the note to 'The Thorn' is continuous with the critique of substitution as a principle of literary language which grounds the revisionary poetics of the 1800 Preface. At first glance, the Preface's rejection of the formulaic 'phrases and figures of speech which from father to son have long been regarded as the common inheritance of Poets' (*PW* I, 132) may imply a similar antipathy towards the speaker who 'cling[s] to the same words', described in the note. Both give instances of language use where associative effects accumulate through repetition: the Preface refers to 'expressions, in themselves proper and beautiful, but which have been foolishly repeated by bad Poets till such feelings of disgust are connected with them as it is scarcely possible by any art of association to overpower' (*PW* I, 132), the note speaks of the 'spirit of fondness, exultation, and gratitude' from which 'the mind luxuriates in the repetition of words which appear successfully to communicate its feelings' (*LB*, 351). In the former instance, however, it is clear that the reiterative habit of the employers of 'what is usually called poetic diction' (*PW* I, 130) has its basis in the assumption that literary language effects the substitution of one set of terms for another, as in the 'curiously elaborate' and periphrastic diction of the Gray sonnet reproduced in this section of the Preface (*PW* I, 132–4). By contrast, the repetition defended in the note stems from the speaker's recognition that the words he repeats could not be exchanged for others with equivalent success. By calling attention to this recognition Wordsworth develops an alternative definition of literary language as dealing in terms which are repeated because irreplaceable.

In the opening passage of a foundational text for late twentieth-century thinking on these tropes, Gilles Deleuze lays out his own distinction between repetition and substitution:

Repetition is not generality. Repetition and generality must be distinguished in several ways. (…) Repetition and resemblance are different in kind — extremely so. (…) [G]enerality expresses a point of view according to which one term may be exchanged or substituted for another. The exchange or substitution of particulars defines our conduct in relation to generality. (…) By contrast, we can see that repetition is a necessary and justified conduct only in relation to that which cannot be replaced. Repetition as a conduct and as a point of view concerns non-exchangeable and non-substitutable singularities. (*DR*, 1)

As a linguistic corollary to this distinction, Deleuze cites the differentiation by the aesthetic writings of Pius Servien, of 'two languages: the language of science, dominated by the symbol of equality, in which every term may be replaced by others; and lyrical language, in which every term is irreplaceable and can only be repeated' (*DR*, 2). We might recall here that Wordsworth, in a footnote to his discussion of poetic diction, proposed that the opposition of 'Poetry and Science' be adopted as 'more philosophical' than the 'contradistinction' of 'Poetry and Prose', which has introduced 'much confusion' into criticism. In the same footnote he asserts that the 'only strict antithesis to Prose is Metre', which, he explains, is only being used in this discussion as 'synonymous' with 'the word "Poetry"' 'against my own judgment' (*PW* I, 134). As with the definition of poetry in the note to 'The Thorn', the shifting substitutions and unsatisfactory equivalences of critical prose throw into relief the 'non-substitutable singularities' of Wordsworth's poetic practice.

ii

Tautologies of various kinds are apparent throughout 'The Thorn'. To read the first stanzas of this disconcerting poem is to be drawn into a complex play of repetition, substitution and difference:

I.

There is a thorn, it looks so old,
In truth you'd find it hard to say,
How it could ever have been young,
It looks so old and grey.
Not higher than a two years' child
It stands erect this aged thorn;
No leaves it has, no thorny points;
It is a mass of knotted joints,
A wretched thing forlorn.
It stands erect, and like a stone
With lichens it is overgrown.

II.

Like rock or stone, it is o'ergrown
With lichens to the very top,
And hung with heavy tufts of moss,
A melancholy crop:
Up from the earth these mosses creep,
And this poor thorn they clasp it round
So close, you'd say that they were bent
With plain and manifest intent,
To drag it to the ground;
And all had join'd in one endeavour
To bury this poor thorn for ever.

Rhyme, a form of verbal repetition that 'includes the difference between two words and inscribes that difference at the heart of a poetic Idea' (*DR*, 21), is encountered here as a recurrent force that, as the Preface to the *Lyrical Ballads* remarks of poetic metre, encourages 'the perception of similitude in dissimilitude' (*PW* I, 148). The rhymed second and fourth lines of the initial quatrains enact, as many readers have observed, the return on the reader's memory of the profoundly familiar four-line ballad stanza, which is subsequently modulated by the 'tail rhyme' of the final six lines.[6] There is a sense of 'redundancy' in the doubling of the seventh line that is dispelled in the closing couplet of each stanza.[7]

The rhymes built into the structure of the stanza are themselves echoed or parodied by the repetitive forms of represented speech in the poem: when the first two lines of stanza II restate the final couplet of the previous stanza, the effect is partly to dilate the phrase, adding 'rock' as an alternative to 'stone', and partly to heighten the chiming end-rhymes of the couplet by collapsing them into a single line. This double rhyme attracts attention to the creeping growth of repetitive sound into surrounding words, in the internal rhyme of 'like' with 'lichen', and of 'or' with 'o'ergrown'. As Deleuze affirms, repetition of single words can be understood as 'generalized rhyme', in which the repeated element 'exercises an attractive force on its neighbours, communicating an extraordinary gravity to them until one of the neighbouring words takes up the baton and becomes in turn a centre of repetition' (*DR*, 21).

The internal rhymes with the particular conjunctions 'or' and 'like' in lines 10–13 also alert us to two dominant principles of tautology in these stanzas and the poem as a whole, namely equivalence and similitude. The first of these principles is apparent in the classic 'belt and braces' formulation of tautology, where two near-synonymous terms are presented as if equivalent or exchangeable, as in the phrases 'rock or stone' (12) and 'plain and manifest' (19). This doubling of terms, however, has the effect of simultaneously hinting at their desynonymization: the extra word is differentiated almost by virtue of its apparent superfluity. The figure of similitude works to similarly ambivalent effect. The unrhymed line 5 offers a negative comparison for the tree: it stands 'Not higher than a two years' child'. Through this circumlocutory expression of likeness the image of the stunted thorn is mapped onto the imaginary figure of an infant, so as metaleptically to suggest that the mosses attempting to 'bury' the tree are reenacting the burial of the baby that may lie beneath the nearby 'hill of moss' (35). But just as the narration shies continually away from finally identifying the hill of moss as a grave, the figure of similitude in the poem holds off from the exchange or substitution of terms that takes place in metaphor.

iii

Defending his assertion that 'repetition and apparent tautology are frequent beauties of the highest kind', Wordsworth alludes to 'innumerable passages from the Bible, and from the impassioned poetry of every nation', citing three examples from the Old Testament:

Awake, awake, Deborah: awake, awake, utter a song: arise Barak and lead thy captivity captive, thou Son of Abinoam.
    At her feet he bowed, he fell, he lay down: at her feet he bowed, he fell: where he bowed there he fell down dead.
    Why is his Chariot so long in coming? Why tarry the Wheels of his Chariot [?] (*LB*, 351)

This association of the principle of repetition with the Old Testament was one definitively established by Robert Lowth's *Lectures on the Sacred Poetry of the Hebrews*, a poetics of the Bible that was to inform the subsequent development of literary criticism in Britain, and of biblical criticism in Europe.[8] The lectures were delivered over the decade (1741–51) during which Lowth held the Chair of Poetry at Oxford University, and were translated from their original Latin in a two-volume edition that appeared in 1787. Wordsworth had read the lectures, in the translation by George Gregory, by the time he wrote the note to 'The Thorn' in September 1800.[9] They are best known today for their formal identification of the structure of the Hebrew prophetic verse with the principle of 'parallelism'. In the nineteenth lecture in the series, entitled 'The Prophetic Poetry is Sententious', Lowth gave the most detailed analysis to date of the patterns discernable in Hebrew versification:

The poetical conformation of the sentences, which has been so often alluded to as characteristic of the Hebrew poetry, consists chiefly in a certain equality, resemblance, or parallelism between the members of each period; so that in two lines (or members of the same period) things for the most part shall answer to things, and words to words, as if fitted to each other by a kind of rule or measure.[10]

    The history of poetical language that develops through Lowth's lectures is manifestly committed to the idea of poetry as a response to God's presence in the universe, whether through the formalized 'responsive' patterns of worship, or, at the moment when poetry was 'first called into existence', through the 'first effort of rude and unpolished verse' returning praise to the Creator, and 'flow[ing] almost involuntarily from the enraptured mind' (*LSP* I, 38). By making poetic inspiration a response to divine inspiration, Lowth here elides the question of the authorship of the biblical verses. Elsewhere in the lectures he alternates between an antiquarian propensity to locate the origins of religious poetry in the earliest Hebrew traditions, and an enthusiastic desire to assert the divine provenance of the Mosaic and prophetic writings: 'Here we may contemplate Poetry in its very beginning; not so much the offspring of human genius, as an emanation from heaven' (*LSP* I, 46).

The 1787 Gregory translation of the *Lectures* reproduces after this last remark a note added to the Göttingen edition by the German biblical scholar Johann David Michaelis. Michaelis takes issue with Lowth's scholarly inconsistency, in 'too carelessly follow[ing] those Jews and Christians, who attribute all the Hebrew writings to the finger of God himself', whilst seeming to 'forget' his 'very just remarks (...) in a succeeding lecture' on the pre-Mosaic origins of Hebrew poetry 'in the choirs of dancers' (*LSP* I, 46–7). The note draws attention to a prevalent tension in Lowth's work, between an historicist attention to the particular context from which the sacred poetry arose, and a pious acknowledgment that, as Scripture, the verses must continue to speak to all ages as the word of God. In so far as he explicitly acknowledges that such a tension exists, Lowth frequently seems to be attempting to resolve it by an appeal to the imaginative sympathy of his audience. In the fifth lecture, 'On the Figurative Style', he proposes that, in order to overcome the 'obstruction' to sympathetic response represented by the historical strangeness of the Hebrews, 'we must even investigate their inmost sentiments, the manner and connexion of their thoughts; in one word, we must see all things with their eyes, estimate all things by their opinions: we must endeavour as much as possible to read Hebrew as the Hebrews would have read it' (*LSP* I, 113).

In order to discourage in his audience the hermeneutic error of 'viewing [Hebrew poetry] from an improper situation, and rashly estimating all things by our own standard' (*LSP* I, 113), Lowth has to reconcile two distinct critical impulses. He has to stress the difference between his contemporary worldview and the extreme 'antiquity' and foreignness of the Hebrews — 'they being the farthest removed from our customs and manners' — whilst simultaneously ensuring that the eighteenth-century reader, 'accustomed to habits of life totally different from those of the [biblical] author', does not suffer a recoil from the strangeness of Hebrew poetry, finding its images 'mean and obscure, harsh and unnatural' (*LSP* I, 112). Lowth bridges this gap by foregrounding the principle of 'resemblance' as the dominant trope of the Hebrew figurative style.

The *Lectures* consider the rhetorical figures of Old Testament verse as conforming almost entirely to this principle of resemblance. The argument is that the earliest forms of poetic language take as illustrative vehicles whatever objects are nearest to hand, and substitute them for the sensations, ideas or emotions they most closely resemble. This substitution is the basis for the figure of metaphor. The Hebrew word for the poetic style, or more generally for poetry itself, *Mashal*, is translated by Lowth as denoting 'resemblance' (*LSP* I, 104). Ian Balfour draws attention to the note inserted at this stage by Lowth's translator, Gregory, reminding the reader that, in fact, 'the associating principle is the true source of figurative language', and that to the category of resemblance must be added those of 'contiguity in time and space' and 'cause and effect' (*LSP* I, 105–6, n. 3), or the principles usually associated with the figure of metonymy. Balfour diagnoses the 'strategic value' of Lowth's almost exclusive emphasis on metaphor as relating to that figure's dependence 'on a natural or motivated resemblance, on an analogy already given in the order of things', as compared with metonymy, which 'can be "motivated" by so arbitrary a relation as mere contiguity, however random or unnatural'.[11]

Lowth acknowledges that, in the absence of a true understanding of the objects originally selected for their qualities of resemblance, a reader's response may be determined by some accident of tempera-ment, or of association. The result in such cases is a response based on aesthetic criteria other than those dictated by historical sympathy:

An opinion of grace and dignity results frequently, not so much from the objects themselves, in which these qualities are supposed to exist, as from the disposition of the spectator, or from some slight and obscure relation or connexion which they have with some other things. Thus it sometimes happens, that the external form and lineaments may be sufficiently apparent, though the original and intrinsic beauty and elegance be totally erased by time. (*LSP* I, 115)

This class of response, proceeding from the 'disposition of the spec-tator', is placed in Lowth's lectures against the more authentic type of response emerging out of a strong imaginative engagement with the historical or geographical position of the Hebrew poets. Lecture Seven, 'Of Poetic Imagery from the Objects of Nature', contains a striking performance of such an engagement. Demonstrating that the prophetic works are filled with metaphors taken from the geographical features of Palestine and the Lebanon, Lowth's commentary itself takes on the characteristics of these natural phenomena: the prophet David, writing on the 'banks of Jordan', 'pours forth the tempestuous violence of his sorrow' (*LSP* I, 133); the poetry of Solomon's Song shares with Mount Carmel its 'rich and fruitful' state, 'abounding with vines, olives, and delicious fruits, (...) displaying a delightful appearance of fertility, beauty and grace' (*LSP* I, 134).

It is, however, clear from the passage succeeding this commentary that Lowth is aware that the situation of some readers does not allow for such a powerfully identificatory response, and that in these cases the deficiency must be supplied by criticism:

In a word, we may generally remark (. . .), that all poetry, and particularly that of the Hebrews, deduces its principal ornaments or imagery from natural objects: and since these images are formed in the mind of each writer, and expressed conformably to what occurs to his senses, it cannot otherwise happen, but, that through diversity of situation, some will be more familiar, some almost peculiar to certain nations; and even those which seem most general, will always have some latent connexion with their immediate origin, and with their native soil. It is the first duty of the critic, therefore, to remark, as far as is possible, the situation and habits of the author, the natural history of his country, and the scene of the poem. Unless we continually attend to these points, we shall scarcely be able to judge with any degree of certainty concerning the elegance or propriety of the sentiments: the plainest will sometimes escape our observation; the peculiar and interior excellencies will remain totally concealed. (*LSP* I, 139–140)

In Lowth's account, the sacred poetry is revealed as historically and geographically distant, operating on a rhetorical principle of resemblance that translates 'through diversity of situation' as difference, and necessitating the interventions of criticism. His insistence that literary tropes originate in the immediate environment of the earliest poets finds a well-known echo in Wordsworth's natural history, in the Preface to the *Lyrical Ballads*, of the fittest language for poetic use, 'arising out of repeated experience and regular feelings' in an idealized agrarian landscape where 'men hourly communicate with the best objects from which the best part of language is originally derived' (*PW* I, 124). The supplementary details provided by the note to 'The Thorn' seemed to some readers to acknowledge that, to borrow Lowth's phrase, 'the peculiar and interior excellencies' of the poem were too definitively, circumstantially located to communicate beyond their immediate context. Francis Jeffrey parodied the note as a 'very peculiar' catalogue of contingencies: ' "Of this piece the reader will necessarily form a very erroneous judgement, unless he is apprised, that it was written by a pale man in a green coat, — sitting cross-legged on an oaken stool, — with a scratch on his nose, and a spelling dictionary on the table." '[12]

Such an insistence on circumstance at once confirms and calls into question the singularity of the literary figure. Those features of the poetry of 'The Thorn' which, alongside its use of repetition, are most frequently singled out as compromising its literary status, are moments when the speaker appears most anxious to be particular. In the third stanza there is scarcely a line where natural objects are not qualified and hedged in with deictic pedantry:

> III.
>
> High on a mountain's highest ridge,
> Where oft the stormy winter gale
> Cuts like a scythe, while through the clouds
> It sweeps from vale to vale;
> Not five yards from the mountain-path,
> This thorn you on your left espy;
> And to the left, three yards beyond,
> You see a little muddy pond
> Of water, never dry;
> I've measured it from side to side:
> 'Tis three feet long, and two feet wide.

The quality that these specifications of time and place share with repetition is their insistent non-exchangeability. In these reductions of the literary to the mathematical figure, the speaker's care that these features of an unnamed landscape (we are directed simply to 'a mountain') should not be mistaken for other trees or ponds challenges and extends almost to the point of absurdity the theory that poetic language is derived from a metaphoric exchange with natural objects, based on a generalized resemblance of concepts. The thorn, the pond and the mossy hill are and yet are not literary signs: they resemble, in their dimensions and locations, the murdered child and its resting place, and yet the repetitive detailing of these dimensions and locations invests them with a quiddity that prevents their assimilation as mere substitutes for mental images. Like the figure of repetition, but unlike metaphor, these signs hint at sameness but deny identity, preserving a sense of dissimilitude in similitude.

iv

Wordsworth's hostility to the pseudo-primitive natural imagery he encountered in Macpherson's *Ossian* suggests an ongoing antipathy to the poetics of substitution:

From what I saw with my own eyes, I knew that the imagery was spurious. In nature, every thing is distinct, yet nothing defined into absolute independent singleness. In Macpherson's work, it is exactly the reverse; every thing (that is not stolen) is in this manner defined, insulated, dislocated, deadened, — yet nothing distinct. It will always be so when words are substituted for things.[13]

By contrast, the note to 'The Thorn' asserts that the beauty of the figure of repetition derives from 'the interest which the mind attaches to words, not only as symbols of the passion, but as *things*, active and efficient, which are of themselves part of the passion' (*LB*, 351). A Lowthian commitment to the origination of tropes in an engagement with natural objects, which nevertheless maintains a critical distance from the idea that figurative language entails the replacement of one term with another, and which simultaneously proposes an emotivist context for figuration, is not easy to sustain. Wordsworth may have encountered all of these positions in Hugh Blair's revision of Lowth's poetics.[14]

Blair's *Lectures on Rhetoric and Belles Lettres*, based on a series delivered at the University of Edinburgh and published in two volumes in 1783, became one of the period's most widely read works on the history and interpretation of figurative language. Blair's intention of 'following the track of that ingenious Author', Robert Lowth, is evident throughout the volumes, but most explicitly acknowledged in Lecture 41, on 'The Poetry of the Hebrews'.[15] Like Lowth, Blair stresses the antiquarian value of the sacred books as 'a curious object of Criticism', and also foregrounds the way that their representation of 'the taste of a remote age and country' (*LRBL* II, 385), requires from the reader an effort of imaginative dislocation:

In order to do justice to [the figurative language of the sacred poetry], it is necessary that we transport ourselves as much as we can into the land of Judæa; and place before our eyes that scenery, and those objects, with which the Hebrew Writers were conversant. (...) For the imagery of every good Poet is copied from nature, and real life; if it were not so, it could not be lively; and therefore, in order to enter into the propriety of his images, we must endeavour to place ourselves in his situation. (*LRBL* II, 392–3)

Where Lowth had identified this act of self-projection as 'the first duty of the critic' whose special knowledge allows him to 'remark' the relevant historical and geographical details (*LSP* I, 140), Blair is more inclined to suggest that 'to transport ourselves' is part of the work of imaginative sympathy carried out by the ordinary reader of such 'remote' literature. This work is necessitated by the mimetic fidelity of the imagery, which can be recognized as 'copied from nature and real life', even if that nature and that life are not those of late eighteenth-century Edinburgh.

In this respect, Blair adapts Lowth's account of the sacred poetry to support his own primitivist agenda. The tendency of 'the Hebrew Writers', 'like every good Poet', to fill their works with imagery copied directly from their immediate environment makes their poetry the greatest, because also the earliest, example of the style of ancient poetry. What Lowth emphasized as the principle of resemblance motivating figuration in ancient Hebrew poetry is also at the forefront of Blair's historical narrative: the Sacred Books are typical of 'the antient original Poets of all nations' (*LRBL* II, 392) in limiting their figurative language to simple and vivid metaphors that 'may be said, not to describe, but to render visible' the objects before them (*LRBL* II, 404). This insistence on the shared stylistic traits between sacred writing and other ancient poetry is part of Blair's contribution through the *Lectures* to a developing poetics of primitivism that would privilege the stylistic characteristics of primary orality, and inculcate in his audience a vigorous response to these vestiges of a pre-literate literature.

To this end, the origin of what Blair pointedly refers to as 'figures of speech' is traced back to a cultural moment before the hegemony of letters: tropes are 'not the inventions of the schools, nor the mere product of study: on the contrary, the most illiterate speak in figures, as often as the most learned' (*LRBL* I, 274). The figures arising from this humble context are, furthermore, differentiated from the 'superfluities and excrescences of Style', which 'were the result of imitation in after times; when Composition passed into inferior hands, and flowed from art and study, more than from native genius' (*LRBL* II, 392). In fact, in the earliest history of language, figures of speech are the product not of copious and extravagant invention but of the 'barrenness' of nomenclature, resulting in a 'want of words' for 'every separate idea'. Under these circumstances, 'men naturally sought to abridge this labour of multiplying words *in infinitum*; and, in order to lay less burden on their memories, made one word, which they had already appropriated to a certain idea or object, stand also for some other idea or object; between which and the primary one, they found, or fancied, some relation' (*LRBL* I, 279).

Metaphor, 'a figure founded entirely on the resemblance which one object bears to another' (*LRBL* I, 295), is therefore revealed as the foundational trope in rhetoric, and the economic utility of transferring meaning between similar objects is identified as the original motivating principle for figurative language. But utility is quickly displaced in Blair's account by an emphasis on the role of the imagination. Figures are deemed to have proliferated because 'there is nothing with which the fancy is more delighted, than with comparisons, and resemblances of objects; and all Tropes are founded on some relation or analogy between one thing and another' (*LRBL* I, 286–7). The original 'barrenness of language, and the want of words', is reassessed as 'not the only, nor, perhaps, even the principal source' of figurative speech: 'tropes have arisen more frequently, and spread themselves wider, from the influence which Imagination possesses over language' (*LRBL* I, 280–1).

Later in the lecture series, Blair continues to modulate his argument on the origin of tropes, moving further away from a Lowthian emphasis on the principle of resemblance, towards a proto-Wordsworthian theory of passion as the source of poetic figures. He argues that the 'most just and comprehensive definition' that can be given of poetry is, ' "That it is the language of passion" ' (*LRBL* II, 312): it follows that the figures employed in poetry are the effect, less of the likenesses between objects, than of the distorted perception resulting from this passion:

Under the influence too of any strong emotion, objects do not appear to us such as they really are, but such as passion makes us see them. We magnify and exaggerate; we seek to interest all others in what causes our emotion; we compare the least things to the greatest; we call upon the absent as well as the present, and even address ourselves to things inanimate. (*LRBL* II, 315)

In this catalogue of rhetorical distortions perceived through the lens of passion, Blair moves his history of language on from the early dependence on 'natural' and mimetic tropes such as metaphor, and incorporates a theory of audience into his account: we resort to figurative language in order to elicit a sympathetic response; because 'we seek to interest all others in what causes our emotion'. Poetry is also associated with early forms of sociality, as exemplified by 'untaught men' 'meeting together in Public Assemblies' (*LRBL* II,

315). It is recognized as the repository for national histories, since 'before Writing was invented', 'Numbers' were necessary to assist the collective memory (*LRBL* II, 316–17).

By contrast, the 'Art of Writing' is an asocial activity undertaken in the solitude of the closet, cut off from the authenticating force of genuine passion and governed by the asymmetrical relations of literary fame:

> In after ages, when Poetry became a regular art, studied for reputation and for gain, Authors began to affect what they did not feel. Composing coolly in their closets, they endeavoured to imitate passion, rather than to express it; they tried to force their imaginations into raptures, or to supply the defect of native warmth, by those artificial ornaments which might give Composition a splendid appearance. (*LRBL* II, 323)

The resemblance to Wordsworth's critique of poetic diction in the 1800 Preface is clear, but the note to 'The Thorn' goes still further, identifying passion as not merely an original motivation, but a continuing component of poetic language: repeated words are of 'themselves part of the passion'. This active participation is dramatized in the poem by Martha's 'doleful cry' (88), ' "O misery! oh misery!/O woe is me! o misery!" ', returning as a refrain to four of the stanzas. It emerges from the narrative that this lament, repeated over 'some two and twenty years' (115) has accumulated the significance of ritual, sustaining as well as expressing the passion felt by the solitary woman.

In a further revision of Blair's theory, Martha's refrain represents a reconciliation of the language of passion with the written word, since the regularity, metrically and recurrently, of its repetition is associated with a 'tempering of the painful feeling which will always be found intermingling with powerful descriptions of the deeper passions' (*PW* I, 150). This mitigating regularity is described in the Preface as an inducement, not, as in Blair, to memory, but to re-reading, since 'of two descriptions either of passions, manners, or characters, each of them equally well executed, the one in prose and the other in verse, the verse will be read a hundred times where the prose is read once' (*PW* I, 150). The foregrounded repetitions of Wordsworth's verse in 'The Thorn' and its accompanying note encourage a re-reading that identifies in the literary text 'a repeatable singularity that depends on an openness to new contexts and therefore on its difference each time it is repeated'.[16]

CORINNA RUSSELL

NOTES

1 Gilles Deleuze, *Difference and Repetition* (1968) (henceforth *DR*), translated by Paul Patton (New York, Columbia University Press, 1994), 1.

2 'Advertisement' to *Lyrical Ballads*, 1798, reprinted in James Butler and Karen Green, editors, *Lyrical Ballads and Other Poems, 1797–1800* (henceforth *LB*) (Ithaca and London, Cornell University Press, 1992), 739.

3 Note to 'The Thorn', *LB*, 351.

4 Frances Ferguson, *Wordsworth: Language as Counter-Spirit* (New Haven and London, Yale University Press, 1977), 11.

5 See, for example, the critique of 'the metrical paraphrases which we have of passages in the Old and New Testament' in the Appendix 'on (. . .) Poetic Diction', *Lyrical Ballads*, 1802, in *The Prose Works of William Wordsworth*, (henceforth *PW*), edited by W. J. B. Owen and Jane Worthington Smyser (Oxford, Clarendon Press, 1974), I, 162–3.

6 See Brennan O'Donnell, *The Passion of Meter: A Study of Wordsworth's Metrical Art* (Kent, Ohio, and London, Kent State University Press, 1995), 133.

7 Thomas Percy, in *Reliques of Ancient English Poetry*, singles out the metre of the ballad 'Sir Cauline' as 'peculiar' on account of the occasional insertion of a 'redundant' 'double third or fourth line' in the stanza (Edinburgh, James Nichol, 1858), I, 31.

8 See Ian Balfour, *The Rhetoric of Romantic Prophecy* (Stanford, Stanford University Press, 2002), and David Norton, *A History of the Bible as Literature*, volume II. (Cambridge, Cambridge University Press, 1993) for details of Lowth's influence on English Romantic poetics, and on the 'Higher Criticism' in Germany.

9 Duncan Wu, *Wordsworth's Reading 1770–1799* (Cambridge, Cambridge University Press, 1993), 89.

10 Lowth, *Lectures on the Sacred Poetry of the Hebrews* (henceforth *LSP*), translated by G. Gregory, 2 volumes (London, J. Johnson, 1787), II, 34. Volume and page numbers henceforth in text.

11 *The Rhetoric of Romantic Prophecy*, 63.

12 *Edinburgh Review*, xii (April 1808), 137, cited in Mary Jacobus, *Tradition and Experiment in Wordsworth's Lyrical Ballads (1798)* (Oxford, Clarendon Press, 1976), 247 n.3.

13 'Essay, Supplementary to the Preface', 1815, *PW* III, 77.

14 Wu's suggested date of reading is 9–26 February 1798. *Wordsworth's reading 1770–1799*, 16.

15 Blair, *Lectures on Rhetoric and Belles Lettres* (henceforth *LRBL*), 2 volumes (London, 1783), II, 386.

16 Derek Attridge, introduction to Jacques Derrida, *Acts of Literature* (Routledge, New York and London, 1992), 14–15.

Ecrire

Ecrire ; serait-ce pour rouvrir sans se lasser ses plaies,
Pour écorcher sa voix, en dedans, davantage,
Ou simple démangeaison de rêveur assagi ?

Tu marches pas à pas à travers tourbillons noircis
Des feux rallumés crépitent au loin, là-bas,
Des rythmes assourdis derrière toi, te harcèlent
C'est la mémoire, vois-tu, la dérangeuse et voyageuse en sus. . .

Or la main a à dire, pour accompagner ton délire
Elle frémit, elle se pose, s'accroche ou va à l'aventure.
Tandis que tu marches à tâtons dans ta nuit
Les mots reviennent soudain comme des lampes.

Aveugle ou cernée, désormais tu écris : plaintes et sanglots
Dans ce soudain silence, se libèrent
Est-ce toi, le rapteur,
Toi aussi, la voleuse de sons,

Râles, rires, berceuses et comptines,
Une main de sorcière les verse dans un puits
Sans fond ou dans quelque prison.
Sur du papier de musique, tes doigts alors
Dessinent des tatouages de rien.

Parfois quelques gouttes de sang giclent de ta main gauche
Ecrire en lettres géantes, ce serait pour qui, pour quoi
Quel cri de nous tous, dans l'infini silence ?

Un seul mot, deux, peut-être
« au secours », « liberté ».
Entre quatre murs, ton sang ainsi séché
Sur de la chaux salie.

Mais tu pourrais aussi écrire le ciel,
l'oiseau dehors.
Ils inonderaient l'ombre de ta cellule.

Dans l'encre perlant de ta peau,
Est-ce la littérature et ses griffures,
Ou le temps éperdu, immobile
La vie s'infiltrant luisante,
Et rouge.

ASSIA DJEBAR, New York 20 mai 2004

Writing

Writing— perhaps to persist in opening old wounds,
Yet again flaying one's voice within
Or just the itchings of a dreamer grown calm?

You pick your way through blackening whirlwinds,
Rekindled fires crackling remotely, from afar
Muffled rhythms behind you, harrying you
It's memory, you see, unsettling, travelling too. . .

But then the hand has things to say, in step with your fever
It flutters, settles, clings tight or flits away.
As you stumble through your night,
Words suddenly return to light your way.

Blind or hemmed in, from now on you write: moans and sobs
Break free in this sudden silence
Are you both raptor
And stealer of sounds? —

Last groans and laughter, cradle songs and rhymes
A witch's hand tips them into a well
A bottomless well or a prison.
And on music paper, your fingers
Start tracing tattoos from thin air.

Sometimes a few drops of blood spurt from your left hand
Writing in giant letters, but for whom, for what
What cry from us all, in the endless silence?

A single word. . . two, perhaps:
'help me', 'freedom'.
Between four walls, your blood now dried
On stained whitewash.

But you could also write the sky,
The bird outside.
They would flood the shadows of your cell.

In the ink beading from your skin
Is it literature and its scratching claws
Or time hurtling, lost, motionless
Life seeping in, gleaming,
Red.

ASSIA DJEBAR, New York 20 May 2004
(Translated by Nicholas Harrison)

Notes on Contributors

Derek Attridge is Professor of English at the University of York and Distinguished Visiting Professor at Rutgers University. Among his books are *The Singularity of Literature* (London and New York, Routledge, 2004), *Peculiar Language: Literature as Difference from the Renaissance to James Joyce* (1988; reissued by Routledge, 2004), and *J. M. Coetzee and the Ethics of Reading: Literature in the Event* (Chicago, Chicago University Press, 2004). He is also the editor of Jacques Derrida's *Acts of Literature* (Routledge, 1992).

Alain Badiou is Professor of Philosophy at the Ecole Normale Supérieure. He is the author of several plays and novels as well as a substantial body of philosophical writing on a wide range of topics. Books translated into English include *Ethics: An Essay on the Understanding of Evil* (London, Verso, 2001), *Saint Paul: The Foundation of Universalism (Cultural Memory in the Present)* (Stanford, Stanford University Press, 2003), *Handbook of Inaesthetics* (Stanford University Press, 2004), and *Theoretical Writings* (London, Continuum, 2004).

Jean Bessière is Professor of Comparative Literature at the Sorbonne Nouvelle Paris III, and Honorary President of the International Comparative Literature Association. His research centres on poetics, rhetoric, and literary theory. Recent books include *La Littérature et sa rhétorique* (Paris, PUF (Presses Universitaires de France), 1999), *Francophonie et postcolonialisme*, co-edited with Jean-Marc Moura (Paris, Champion, 2001) and *Quel statut pour la littérature?* (Paris, PUF, 2001). A new book, *Principes de la théorie littéraire*, is due out with PUF in September 2005.

Assia Djebar has written poetry and directed films but is best known as the author of more than a dozen novels and collections of prose writing in French. Her works have been translated into numerous languages; in English they include *Women of Algiers in their Apartment* (Charlottesville, University Press of Virginia, 1992), *Fantasia: An Algerian Cavalcade* (London, Quartet, 1989), *Algerian White* (New York, Seven Stories, 2001). Her most recent novel is *La Disparition de la langue française* (Paris, Albin Michel, 2003). She is currently Silver Professor of French and Francophone Studies at New York University.

Nicholas Harrison is currently Senior Lecturer in the French department at University College London, and from September 2005 will be Reader in French at King's College London. He is the author of two books, *Circles of Censorship: Censorship and its Metaphors in French History, Literature and Theory* (Oxford, Clarendon, 1995) and *Postcolonial Criticism: History, Theory and the Work of Fiction* (Cambridge, Polity, 2003).

Simon Jarvis teaches English at the University of Cambridge. He is the author of books on the history of editing and on Adorno and is currently completing a study of poetic thinking in Wordsworth.

Benita Parry is Honorary Professor in the Department of English and Comparative Literary Studies at the University of Warwick. Her work in postcolonial studies and on the literature of Empire began with her book *Delusions and Discoveries: Studies on India in the British Imagination, 1880–1930*, published in 1972 and republished in a revised edition in 1998 (London, Verso). Her second book was *Conrad and Imperialism: Ideological Boundaries and Visionary Frontiers* (London, Macmillan, 1983), and her most recent, *Postcolonial Studies: A Materialist Critique*, was published by Routledge in 2004.

Jacques Rancière is Emeritus Professor at the University of Paris VIII (St-Denis). Much of his work has centred on the connections between aesthetics, politics and philosophy; his many publications, most of which have been translated into English, include *The Names of History: On the Poetics of Knowledge* (Minnesota University Press, 1994), *On the Shores of Politics* (Verso, 1995), *The Flesh of Words: The Politics of Writing (Atopia: Philosophy, Political Theory, Aesthetics)* (Stanford University Press, 2004) and *The Politics of Aesthetics: The Distribution of the Sensible* (London, Continuum, 2004).

Corinna Russell is College Lecturer and Director of Studies in English at Emmanuel College, Cambridge. She has interests in the Romantic and Victorian periods and is working on a study of the rhetoric of redundancy, repetition, tautology and gratuitousness in nineteenth-century definitions of the literary. Her publications include the chapter on the novel in *Romanticism: An Oxford Guide* (2005), and an essay, ' "A Fine Excess": Hopkins, Keats, and the Gratuity of Grace' in a forthcoming collection, *Religion and Romanticism from William Cowper to Wallace Stevens* (London, Ashgate).